D1029092

CONTEMPORARY JAPANESE HOUSES

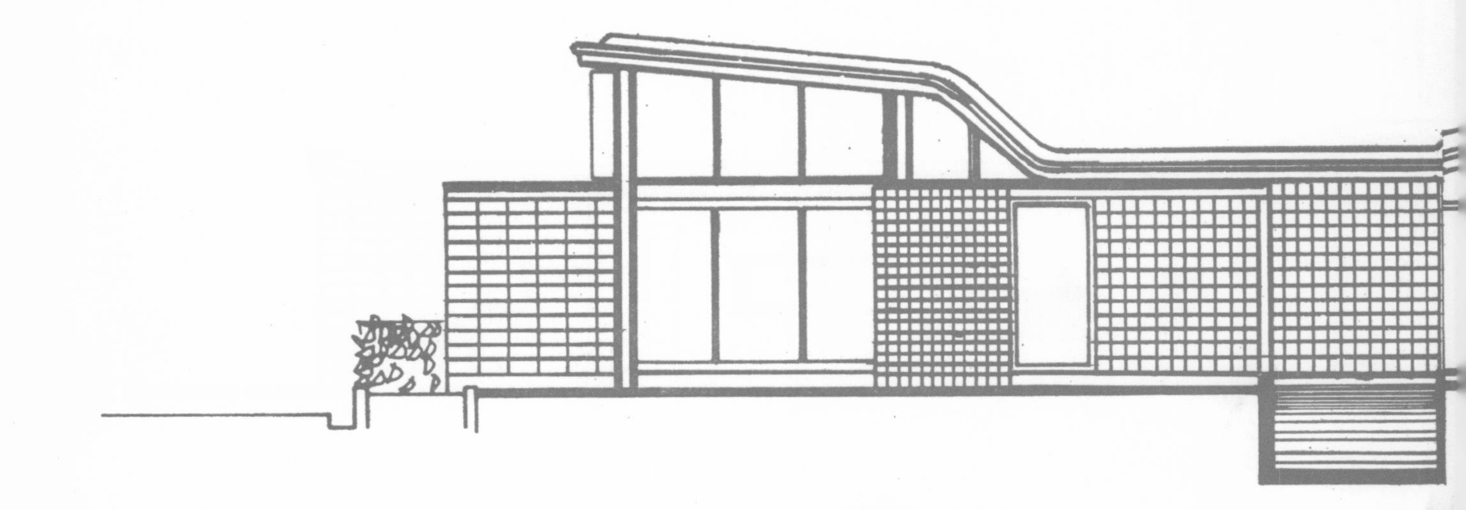

CONTEMPORARY

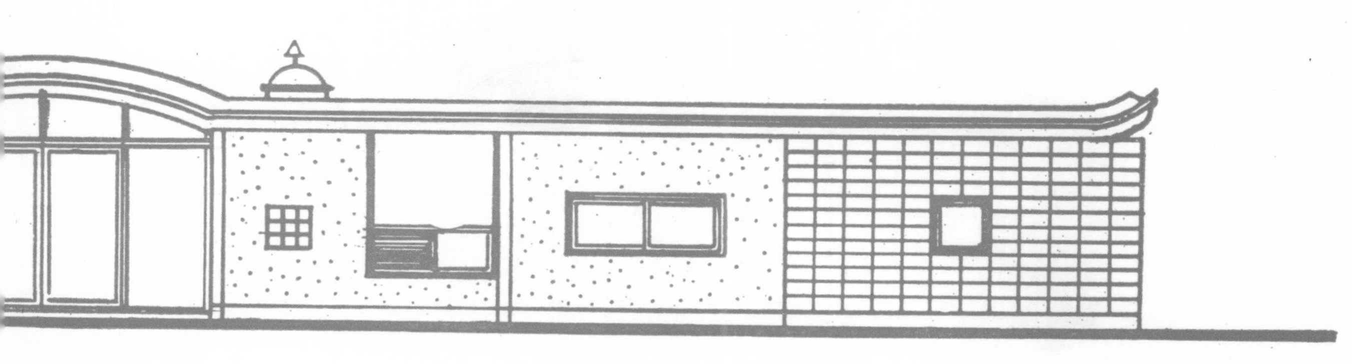

JAPANESE HOUSES

Vol. 2

CHARLES S. TERRY

KODANSHA INTERNATIONAL LTD:

TOKYO, JAPAN & PALO ALTO, CALIF., U.S.A.

DISTRIBUTORS:

British Commonwealth (excluding Canada and the Far East)
WARD LOCK & COMPANY LTD.
London and Sydney

Continental Europe
BOXERBOOKS, INC.
Zurich

The Far East
JAPAN PUBLICATIONS TRADING COMPANY
C.P.O. Box 722, Tokyo

Published by KODANSHA INTERNATIONAL LTD., 2-12-21, Otowa, Bunkyo-ku, Tokyo, Japan and KODANSHA INTERNATIONAL/USA, LTD., 577 College Avenue, Palo Alto, California 94306. Printed in Japan.

Library of Congress Catalog No. 64–25254
SBN 87011–051–9; JBC 1052–780508–2361

First edition, 1968
Second printing, 1969

TABLE OF CONTENTS

PREFACE

AS IN *the first volume of* Contemporary Japanese Houses, *the houses presented in this book were selected by a process of elimination. Limiting myself to houses completed during the interval between mid-1964 and mid-1967, I first picked out approximately seventy-five outstanding examples and then pared that number down to twenty, attempting to arrive at the widest possible range of types, while presenting only the best house in any given type. This method was dictated to a large extent by my wish to give full pictorial coverage to each house but at the same time avoid redundancy of ideas. I have made no attempt actually to classify the houses, but I believe the reader will see that they fall into categories ranging from "small, urban, low-cost, traditional" to "large, country, expensive, Western" with numerous variations in between. Whether I have succeeded in selecting the best house in each type is, of course, a matter of question, and I can only beg that selections of this sort are bound to be to some extent subjective.*

This book is directed primarily at Occidental readers, some of whom will be familiar with modern Japan and some of whom will not. While trying not to belabor the obvious, I have nevertheless included a good deal of background information that will be old hat to those who are experienced with Japan and its contemporary culture, my hope having been to make the book intelligible to other readers who need to be told, for example, where the Izu Peninsula is.

I am grateful to the following architects for supplying me not only with plans and drawings, but with statements as to the intentions of their designs: Mr. Tadayoshi Fujiki, Mrs. Masako Hayashi, Mr. Tetsuya Hayashi, Mr. Tatsuya Hirobe, Mr. Tsutomu Ikuta, the Design Department of Kajima Construction Company, Mr. Dan Miyawaki, Miss Nobuko Nakahara, Mr. Tadashi Okamura, Mr. Antonin Raymond, the RIA Group, Mr. Junzō Sakakura, Mr. Kiyosi Seike, Mr. Seiichi Shirai, Mr. Shin Takaya, the Design Department of Takenaka Construction Company, Mr. Kamon Tatehata, Mr. Akio Yamamoto, and Mr. Junzō Yoshimura.

I am also grateful to Mr. David Leavitt, who conferred with me several times during the selection of the houses and offered many valuable suggestions; to Mr. Hidetoshi Yajima, who performed the arduous task of preparing the architectural drawings for publication; and to Mr. Masakazu Kuwata, who devoted much thought, care, and skill to the layout of the book.

I would like to express my special gratitude to Mrs. Yoshiko Nihei, without whose expert assistance this book could not have been prepared. Mrs. Nihei not only helped with the selection and acquisition of photographs, but checked out countless details and maintained liaison with the designers and owners of the houses, the various photographers whose pictures were used, and the staff members in charge of the book at Kodansha International. Though she is in no way responsible for the choice of the houses or the opinions expressed concerning them, it would not be too much to say that she gathered together the numerous pieces from which the book was made.

Finally, I would like to thank Mrs. Michio Ihara and Mr. Charles Pomeroy for their careful editing of the book and for their patience in dealing with an author who, to put it mildly, has a tendency to be tardy.

CHARLES S. TERRY

Tokyo
August 3, 1967

INTRODUCTION

THERE IS no need to repeat here the comments made in the first volume of *Contemporary Japanese Houses* on the subject of traditional and present-day Japanese housing, but it does not seem superfluous to stress once again the rapidity with which the Japanese concept of a comfortable dwelling has been and is still changing. Indeed, a comparison of the houses in the earlier volume with the ones presented here will show a number of important developments that have occurred in the three short years that separate the books.

It goes without saying that the houses shown here are exceptional, if only because they were all designed by architects, whereas a large majority of the private houses built in Japan are put together by owners and carpenters. Consequently, it cannot be said that the ways of life represented by the designs shown here are entirely typical of the modern Japanese scene. At the same time, it is virtually axiomatic that houses designed by competent architects for people sufficiently sophisticated to engage them are pacemakers, quick to reflect subtle changes in manners and custom, and quick also to be imitated by other people who have been vaguely wondering how to accommodate their dwellings to these changes.

The changes themselves are often only half-perceived by the majority of people or even by the mass media of public information. For example, every Japanese who watches television—this includes nearly everybody—must have noticed that he sees a lot more beds than he used to. The eminently up-to-date action-movie hero who poses for the whiskey commercial does not sleep on the tatami, he has a bed. He *has* to have a bed, or else, to put it bluntly, he would not be able to sell the whiskey, because beds have become a part of the "image" of modern living. And yet very few people have commented in public on the rapid increase in the use of beds in Japan, and nobody seems to have observed that the introduction of this large piece of furniture will without doubt eventually change the prevailing concept of what a room for sleeping should be, both in size and in overall design. Until not very many years ago there was a widespread belief that the Japanese slept on mattresses on the tatami because they preferred these to beds, but the growing sales of beds in the country suggest that the preference, if it actually existed, was dictated at least in part by the lack of anything other than mattresses and tatami to sleep on.

The effect of the adoption of beds on the design of houses is perhaps even greater than that of the gradual introduction of chairs, tables, and other Western furnishings, because a bed, while increasing the minimal acceptable size of the bedroom, at the same time prevents it from doubling as a sitting room, as it did in the past. Young Japanese couples who do not feel terribly cramped in two-room apartments so long as they sleep on the floor begin, when they consider acquiring a bed, to feel the need for three rooms. One wonders, indeed, what is to become of the ubiquitous government and private apartment houses now being built, in which the customary unit (called the "2DK," which signifies two small rooms and a dining-kitchen) does not really have enough room for a double bed. If the rise in the Japanese standard of living continues at the same pace as in the past fifteen years, these buildings will doubtless be obsolete in another few years anyway, but the increasing demand for beds is certain to hasten their obsolescence. (Many would argue that they would have been obsolete from the beginning, but for the acute housing shortage.)

It was pointed out in the earlier volume of this book that many of the chairs and sofas encountered in Japanese houses were rarely sat in and were consequently allowed less space than they might seem to a Western eye to require. The impression left by the houses in this volume, however, is that in the last two or three years, people have grown more accustomed to sitting in chairs or on sofas even when at leisure. The result is that living rooms are beginning to acquire a less stiff and more comfortable appearance than in the past. Furnishings in general lag behind those of Europe and America in style and in quality, but any Occidental resident of Japan would testify that they have improved vastly in the past few years. The underlying cause is no doubt the increasing demand for good furniture and the growing willingness on the part of the public to pay the necessary cost. At the same time, the improvement in quality has helped to stimulate demand. It is a two-way reaction.

It was noted in the earlier volume that one of the great problems with which Japanese house designers have to deal is the necessity of having not only a Western-style living room where guests are received, but a Japanese-style living room where the occupants actually live. As more and more people acquire the habit of sitting in chairs even when company is not present, it becomes possible to eliminate the Japanese-style living room and enlarge the Western-style room. This is actually what has happened in a good many of the houses presented here, with the result that on the whole the floor plans shown are less cluttered than those in the first volume. In one or two instances, the opposite has occurred: the Western-style living room has either been left out entirely or treated more frankly as a space for receiving guests and nothing more. The effect is still that the plan becomes cleaner and more definite in purpose. In a way, the very elimination of excessively small living rooms indicates an increased understanding of Occidental furnishings, for it suggests that people who cannot bring themselves to part with tatami have come to realize that it is better to have no Western living room at all than to have one that is too crowded.

What is perhaps a more startling evidence of change than the elimination of either Western-style living rooms or tatami living rooms is the presence in some of the larger houses shown here of *two* Western-style living rooms, one of which is an informal family sitting room. Here is the surest indication of all that the chair is being accepted as something other than an instrument of torture. In the houses presented in 1964, where there were two living rooms, one was Western, and one was Japanese. The suspicion was voiced at that time that in such instances the owners probably considered the Japanese room the more comfortable. In the houses shown here, however, spaces that might have been occupied by tatami rooms are in fact occupied by Western rooms, and the clear implication is that more and more people actually prefer chairs to tatami, just as they prefer beds to tatami and mattresses.

Certain Japanese traditions remain sacred. No matter how Western the house, people still remove their shoes upon entering, and it remains necessary to provide, even in the smallest houses, an entranceway where shoes can be taken off and stored. There is doubtless a small possibility that even a people long accustomed to the clean and comfortable custom of walking about the house barefoot or in their stockinged feet will have the temerity to abandon it in favor of clomping about in shoes, but it seems rather more likely, humans being humans, that the opposite will occur, and architects in countries other than Japan would perhaps be well advised to study the Japanese treatment of the entrance hall.

On the other hand, the hitherto nearly religious separation of the toilet from the bath appears gradually to be breaking down, no doubt because toilets are now much more sanitary than they once were. One large manufacturer has even begun to market a bath-toilet unit for apartments and small houses. Still, the Japanese mode of bathing, which involves splashing water all over the bathroom, while using the tub for soaking only, tends to make the combination of toilet and bath difficult, even though economical.

In looking through this book, the reader will probably notice that to a greater extent than in the previous book, the pictorial emphasis is on the details and the interiors rather than on the overall external appearance of the houses. One reason is simply that in some instances the surrounding area was so crowded that there was no vantage point from which to photograph the exterior as a whole. A more important reason, however, is the development of a new genre of town houses in which the exterior—which is to say, the face presented to the public—is relatively unimportant. It will be noted, of course, that these two reasons are related, for if there is no vantage point from which to photograph an exterior, there is no vantage point from which to look at it, and consequently it ceases to have as much aesthetic importance as it would otherwise have. In the jam-packed cities of present-day Japan this is a situation that arises with increasing frequency.

It is currently estimated that about half of the residents of Tokyo and Osaka, Japan's two largest cities, live in apartment houses that are to all intents and purposes a postwar development. It remains true, however, that most Japanese prefer a small house with a garden to an apartment, and one result is that even in downtown areas where land for private houses would seem prohibitively expensive, private houses remain, and new ones are being built all the time. Urban land has been atomized, in the sense that a vast number of landowners cling jealously to an equally vast number of small plots, and these are typically in areas where the government has not succeeded in acquiring enough space for anything more than the narrowest conceivable streets. The very multiplicity of land ownership militates against urban redevelopment in countless districts, and, as a consequence, private residences continue to go up in areas that would doubtless better be served by high-rise apartment houses.

Owing to this situation, Japanese architects are constantly required to design town houses for sites that are desirable only because of their central location. Quite frequently the main problem is to create a comfortable residence on a plot that is really too small for it, facing on a street that is too narrow, and surrounded by other houses that are also on plots that are too small for them, facing on streets that are also too narrow, and so on. In such circumstances, it is inevitable that the insurance of privacy and comfort takes precedence over the external appearance of the building.

Some years ago a prominent Japanese architect designed a town house that he called a "House with No Front." There *was*, of course, a front, but it was little more than a blank concrete wall separating the interior from the street before the house. Within, rooms alternated with inner courts in a plan that preserved the traditional openness of Japanese houses and brought to mind the concept of the atrium in ancient Roman houses. Several interpretations of this general idea will be found among the houses presented here, and it seems certain that unless land-ownership patterns in the cities change, more and more inner-directed houses will appear.

A second kind of building designed for small plots in densely populated areas is the multistory house—a type that developed in Western cities more than a century ago, but remained rare in Japan until recently because of the lack of other building materials than wood. Only one example is presented in this book, but it seems likely that three- and four-story houses will gradually become more numerous, perhaps as a transition toward the genuine high-rise apartment houses that would solve the urban housing problems. It will be observed that the single example shown here reveals an effort to preserve the garden and the outdoor living space that the Japanese so love.

Of the houses shown here, thirteen were built as ordinary residences in the city or suburbs, six are out-and-out country houses, and one is a country house that in the future will be used as a year-round dwelling. It should not be assumed from these figures that roughly a third of the houses built in Japan are country houses. On the contrary, such houses represent only a small fraction of the total, though it does seem, in the absence of statistics, that the number of people in Japan who have country houses is proportionately larger than in most countries of the West, partially because of the proximity of suitable seaside and mountainside areas to the cities, and partially because land in the country is immensely cheaper than land in the city. Many Japanese families who live in small apartments because they cannot afford their own houses in the city can at least manage a small house in the country to which they can retreat on weekends and holidays.

Plots for country houses are normally larger than for urban houses, and the architects who design the houses consequently have greater freedom. Too, since these are occasional residences, the designers are apt to be somewhat more daring than when they are working on ordinary houses. A coincidental, but felicitous, result is that the buildings they produce often turn out to be highly imaginative creations that would fit beautifully into suburban settings in other countries, or for that matter, in Japan itself, if the price of suburban land were not so inflated by the urban sprawl as to make truly spacious plots forbiddingly expensive for most people. A number of the country houses shown here would, with minor adjustments, make excellent year-round dwellings in, say, the outer reaches of Los Angeles or the suburbs of New York.

The houses shown in this book range in price from about $3,000 to nearly $300,000. An effort has been made here to indicate how much each house actually costs, but since the price of materials and labor tends to increase as the years pass, the estimated costs listed can by no means be taken as exact figures. They are intended simply as a rough guide as to what a similar house might cost in Japan at the present time and, even more, as an indication of the budget with which the designers were working. The general purpose of this book is not to suggest patterns for "graceful living," but rather to show architectural methods that have been devised to meet specific problems under specific conditions. One of the most important specific conditions (and often the most important specific problem) is the budget available for the building, and it would be unobjective not to give some idea of its size. At the same time, it should be emphasized that the figures are not absolute, but relative. They show, in brief, whether the designer had a small, medium, or large amount of money at his disposal.

CONTENTEMPORARY JAPANESE HOUSES

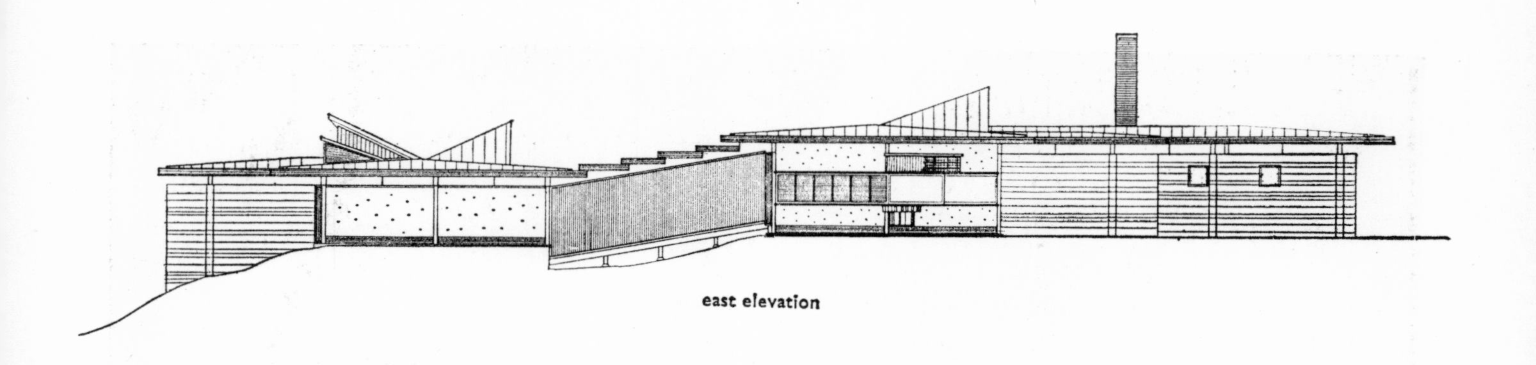

east elevation

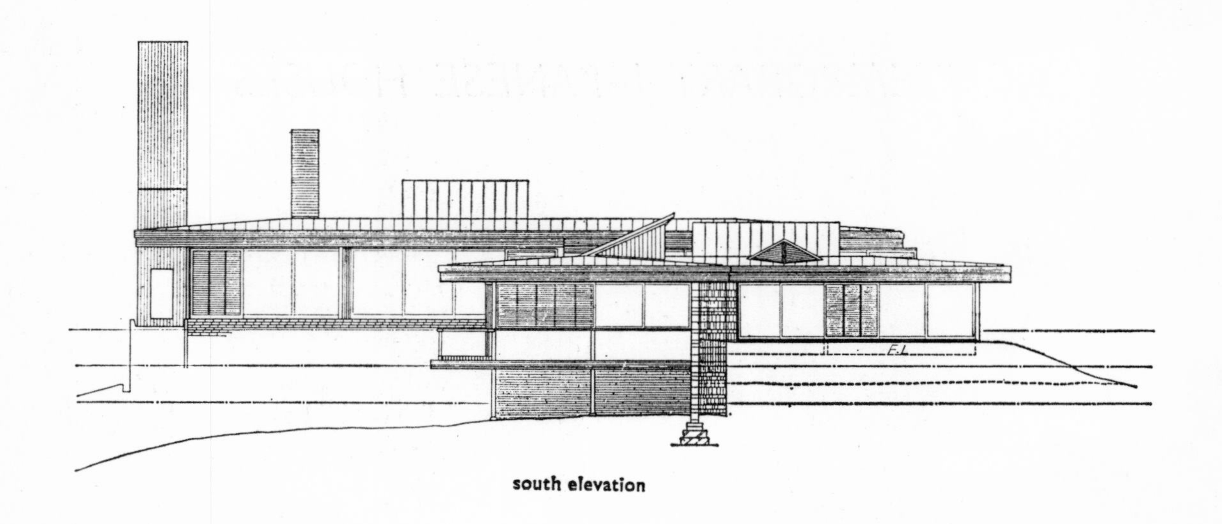

south elevation

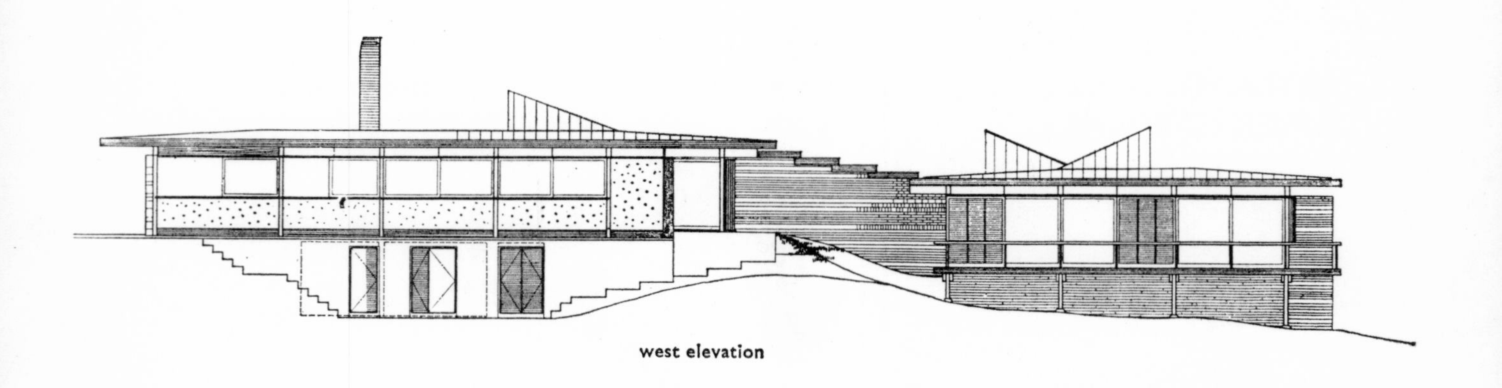

west elevation

SKYLIGHTS AND INNER GARDENS

Architects: Junzō Sakakura Design Research Center
Location: Nishinomiya, Hyōgo Prefecture
Builders: Masumi Construction Co.
Garden: Fukunaga Gardening Co.
Site area: 22,649 square feet
Building area: 2,802 square feet
Floor area: 2,948 square feet
Estimated cost: $52,780.00

THE DESIGNERS of this charming wood-and-brick building are noted, among other things, for their town houses with inner courts, or atriums, intended for urban areas where a house that opens in upon itself is apt to be more peaceful than one directed toward the exterior. In this instance, the site was a spacious wooded lot in the outskirts of Osaka, and there was no need for a closed plan, but excellent use was made of the inner-court concept (*see* §1, §7, *and floor plan*).

The traditional Japanese separation of public and private quarters is carried to its logical conclusion here. The bedroom section is, in effect, a separate building linked to the more public part of the house only by a hallway (§8). Since the bedroom area is on lower ground than the living and dining rooms, the hall becomes a sort of stairway, and the gradual change in level is articulated in its roof (*see* §4, §7, *and elevation*). Between the two sections of the house are semi-closed courts that provide most of the rooms with a view of well-manicured garden areas. In a larger sense, the designers have arranged to have all of the principal rooms open on two sides, so as to achieve maximum contact between indoors and outdoors.

The land slopes from the northeast to the southwest, and the house has the benefit of the cool breezes that come from the west in this vicinity in the summer. There is a view of the ocean in this direction, and the designers have carefully made it available to all rooms on the west side of the building, while at the same time preserving the customary openness of the south side.

As is so often the case in Japan, the house is occupied by three generations: the owner and his wife, their two grown children, and the owner's mother. The two younger generations sleep in beds and consequently have Western-style bedrooms, but the mother prefers a traditional Japanese suite on the east side of the house, which has a garden in near-traditional style (§7). Guests of the reigning middle generation ordinarily enter through the large entrance hall (§2), but the mother and the children are able to have their friends come to their parts of the house directly through the garden, if they choose.

A small inner court by the side of the entrance hall provides cross-ventilation for the living room and kitchen and, at the same time, serves as a kind of front porch. The living room (COLOR §§1 & 2; §7) is provided with extra light by a large skylight, as are the bath, toilet, and hallway in the bedroom section. The skylights, particularly the one in the living room, add a new dimension to the spatial variety of the interior.

The linking of exterior and interior is a dominant theme in this house. The brick wall of the central hallway extends into the living room and is repeated in the entrance hall, from which it again emerges outside (§§2 & 7). The dining room (§5), for its part, is linked with its terrace (§6) by clinker-tile flooring, which incidentally facilitates panel floor heating in the interior. And as is characteristic of the Sakakura group, a great tree is allowed to grow out of the terrace up through the extended eaves (§1)—a touch reminiscent of the earlier "Neo-Japanese House," which appeared in the first volume of *Contemporary Japanese Houses* (pp. 119–128).

◁ COLOR §*1 A large skylight facing north provides additional light, as well as spatial variation, in the living room.*

§1 A sloping lawn separates the wing containing the children's bedrooms, whose veranda is visible in the foreground, from the living and dining rooms. The interruption of the eaves over the terrace to make way for a large tree helps to bring the house and its natural surroundings more closely together. ▷

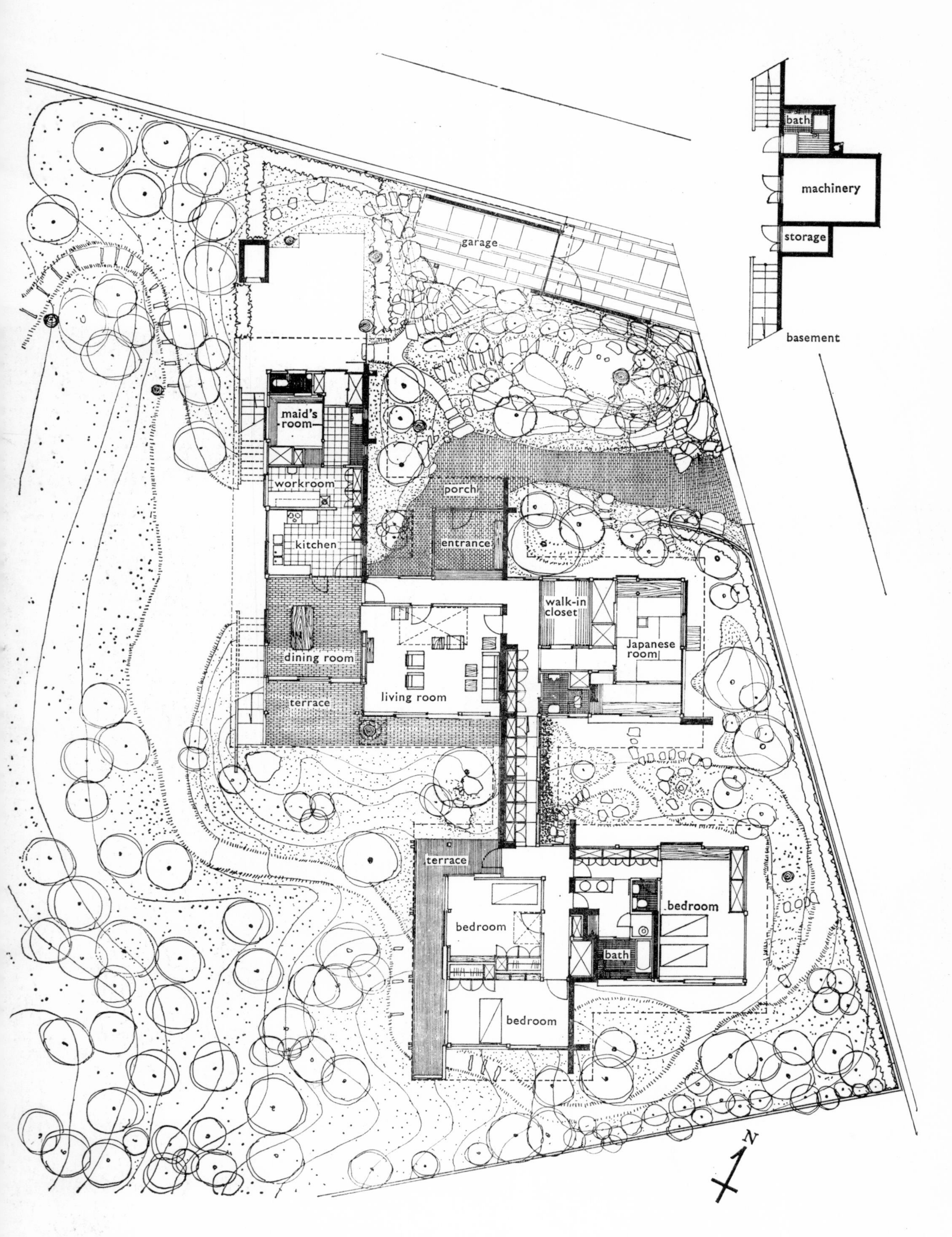

garage
maid's room
workroom
porch
entrance
kitchen
walk-in closet
Japanese room
dining room
living room
terrace
terrace
bedroom
bedroom
bath
bedroom
bath
machinery
storage
basement
N

§2 *A unity of building materials is preserved throughout the house. The ceiling and brick wall of the large entrance hall are repeated in the living room, and the clinker-tile floor appears again in the dining room and terrace.*

§3 The east wall of the living room extends to form the outer wall of the stairway-hall, thus creating an architectural link between interior and exterior. The same brick wall appears again in the entrance hall, from which it once again projects outside the house.

COLOR §2 *The southeast side of the living room has broad glass doors that look out on a semi-enclosed garden. The color scheme of solid primary and pastel hues harmonizes with the burnt-brick wall on the east side of the room.*

§4 A black-lacquered partition separates the living room from the dining room. The kitchen and utility wing, not visible here, extend to the right of the dining room.

§5 The clinker-tile paving of the terrace is brought inside to form the floor of the dining room, underneath which there is panel heating. In the distance at left-center is the veranda of the children's wing.

§6 Like all the other main rooms of the house, the living room (left-center) has openings on two sides. The living room, dining room, and covered terrace form one large integrated space in which there is a gradual transition from interior to exterior. The bedroom section at far right is about three feet lower than the living-dining area.

§7 A suite on the east side of the house, which is occupied by the owner's mother, looks out on a secluded garden containing a "sea" of white gravel and several grassy knolls representing islands. The wall and skylight beyond the garden belong to the master bedroom. At right-center is a repetition of the projecting brick-wall theme. In effect, the brick partitioning forms a central axis for the house, marking off the public spaces from the private, while at the same time delineating three distinct spaces within the private area.

§8 The stairway-hall is lined on the right side with glass doors and on the left with closets. The door at the far end of the photograph opens on the north garden and serves as a separate entrance to the mother's suite.

§9 Four skylights project from the L-shaped roofs and a rectangular opening is located over a small court between the entrance hall and the kitchen.

HOUSE AND ATELIER FOR A PAINTER

Architect: Kiyosi Seike
Location: Seijō, Tokyo
Builders: Okada Construction Co.
Site area: 7,492 square feet
Building area: 2,180 square feet
Estimated cost: $22,220.00

LOCATED IN one of the quieter residential districts of Tokyo, this house doubles as a residence and working place for a prominent painter. The site is long on the east-west axis, and the designer adopted the straightforward tactic of making a long, narrow house near the north border with as ample a garden as possible on the south (§11). The atelier, which also serves as an office, is on the west end, near the street (§10), and the living quarters (§12) are at the east end, where disturbances from without are minimal. The "interchange" between these two sections is an entrance hall opening on the north. Starting from the south wall of the entrance hall, a long rectangular pond not only completes the division of the two sections of the house, but separates the house garden from the atelier garden (§12 & COLOR §3).

The lot is slightly higher on the east end than on the west, and the floor of the residential area was accordingly raised about eight inches above that of the atelier section. Thanks to this difference and to the curving sculptured roof, it was possible to adjust the ceiling heights of the various rooms to their particular functions, giving the atelier a high ceiling with clerestory windows and the living quarters a lower ceiling that arches slightly over the living-dining room (§§15 & 16).

Since artists no longer demand light from the north only, the architect made the atelier quite open on the south, where a covered terrace forms a transition between the interior and the garden (§14). In the summer the owner-artist can work in the atelier, on the terrace, or in the garden, dependent upon the weather and his lighting requirements. The three sections actually compose a single space with varying light conditions.

Although one of the aims of the design was to separate the artist's working area from his house, the residential area contains a small study where he can read or work out designs in private (§18). This has a charming floor-level window through which he can see a diminutive enclosed garden on the north, itself planned primarily as an adjunct to a Japanese bedroom in the innermost part of the house (§17).

The designer, Kiyosi Seike, has likened the building, on the one hand, to a railroad train, and, on the other, to a Japanese picture scroll, which tells its story from left to right as one unrolls it. The house is certainly more beautiful than a railroad train, and probably more serviceable. Whether one considers it as beautiful as a picture scroll depends to a large extent on whether one judges buildings by their prettiness or by the architectural ingenuity and integrity that they reveal. By the latter criterion, this house is indeed a thing of beauty.

◁ COLOR *§3 On the south side of the atelier there is a semi-closed terrace leading to a garden which is separated from the garden outside the residential section by a long rectangular pond. The pond intrudes into the house as far as the glass-brick back wall of the entrance hall. The atelier, its terrace, and its garden were conceived as an integrated indoor-outdoor working space in which the artist-owner has a wide choice of lighting conditions.*

§10 The atelier, which is closest to the street, has clerestory windows on three sides, with a brise-soleil on the east. Behind the concrete-block wall at the right is a series of three storage rooms. ▷

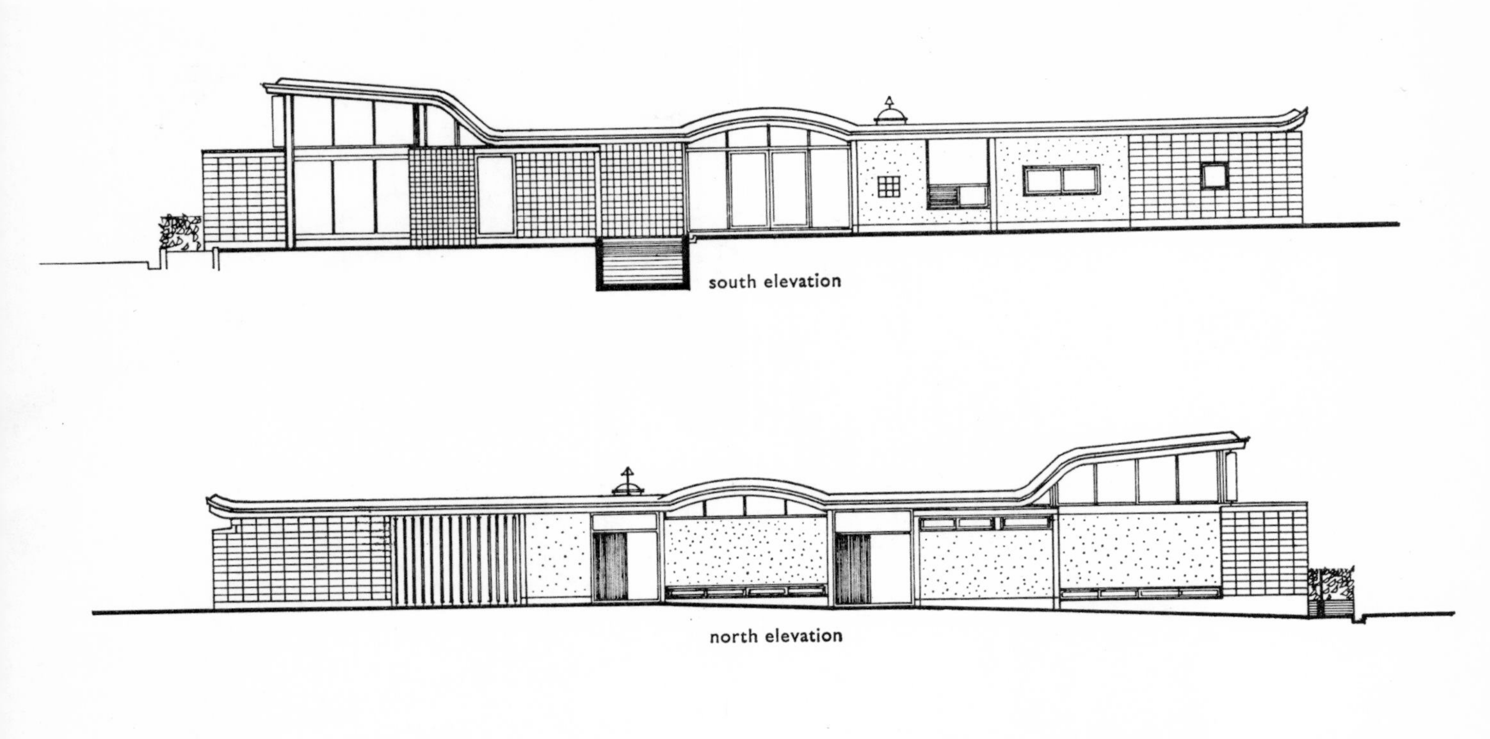

south elevation

north elevation

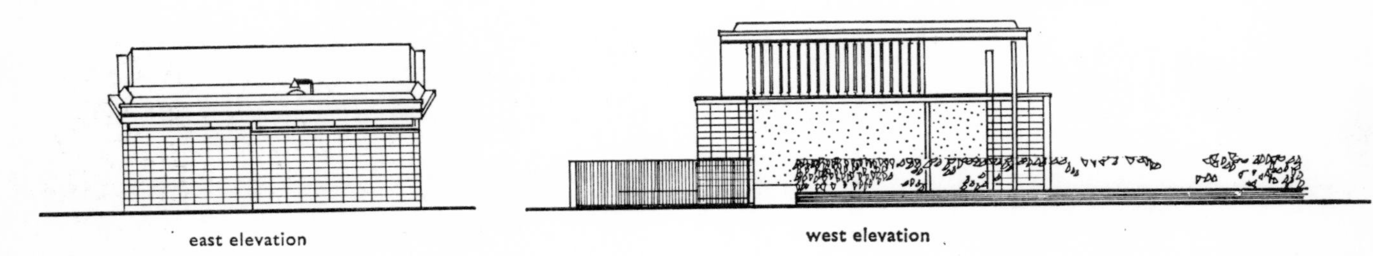

east elevation

west elevation

§12 The arched roof of the living-dining room marks the begining of the residential section, which is at a slightly higher ground level than the atelier and consequently has lower ceilings. The bedrooms are appropriately placed at the farthest end of the house, where they are as remote as possible from street noises.

§11 Seen form the southeast, the house resembles a railway train. The upward-thrusting hood of the atelier and the arch over the living room add movement and plasticity to the otherwise flat roof.

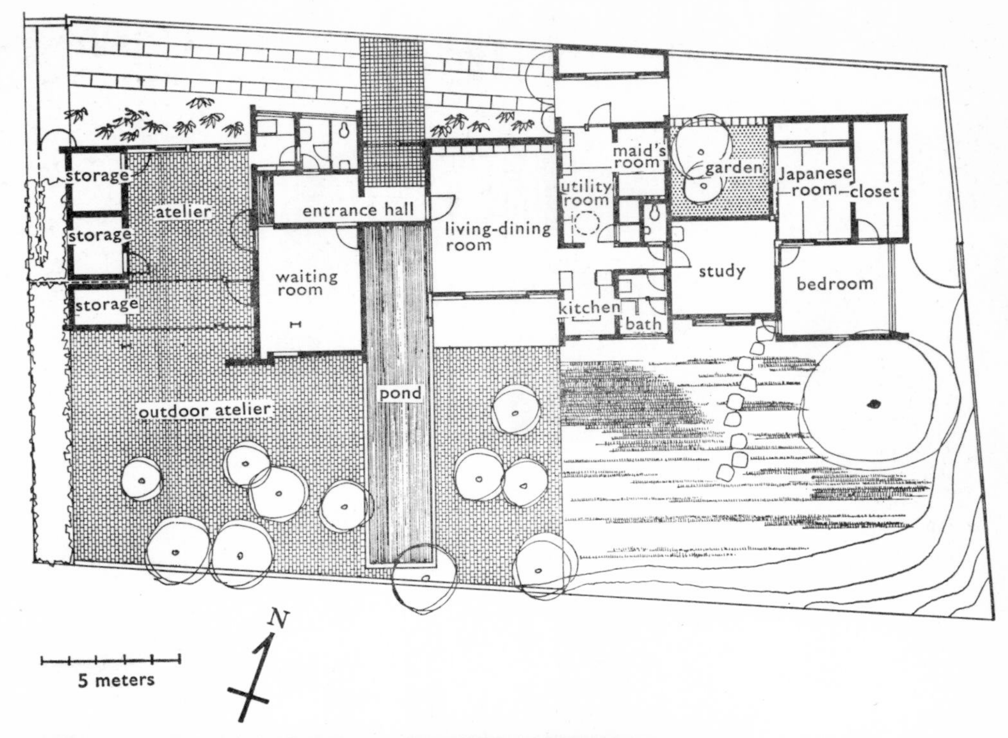

§13 The view is from the entrance hall toward the waiting room outside the atelier. The wall behind the bench reaches only partway to the ceiling and light is admitted from the clerestory windows of the atelier behind.

§14 The brick floor of the atelier extends out to the terrace and garden, creating a strong link between interior and exterior. The doors at the right lead to storage rooms. ▷

§15 The arched roof permits a higher ceiling in the living-dining room than in the other parts of the residential section. The living room has full floor-to-ceiling openings on the south and west sides.

§16 The north end of the living-dining room is occupied by a multipurpose shelf, which does not quite block the view of the exterior. The door at the left leads to the entrance hall.

§17 The Japanese-style bedroom at the east end of the house looks out on a small rock-and-gravel garden, which is cut off from the exterior on the north by vertical louvers.

§18 The small study in the residential section has waist-level windows facing on the main garden. On the opposite side of the room, floor-level windows look out on the lower part of the garden shown in §17.

HOUSE NEAR THE FIELDS

Architect: Kiyosi Seike
Location: Shizuoka, Shizuoka Prefecture
Builders: Kurebayashi Construction Co.
Site area: 9,942 square feet
Building area: 1,700 square feet
Total floor area: 2,367 square feet
Estimated cost: $20,830.00

SHIZUOKA, the capital of Shizuoka Prefecture, is about 120 miles southwest of Tokyo. It is on the Tokaido Line and appears destined eventually to become a subcenter in the Tokyo-Nagoya-Osaka megalopolis, but at present it has a population of only about 400,000 and may be considered a typical Japanese provincial city. The house shown here is on the outskirts of Shizuoka, in an enviable spot where there is a bucolic view of rice fields and a fair-sized river to the south (§19).

The occupants are a typical Japanese family of four—husband, wife, and two school-age children—who commute to Shizuoka for work, school, or shopping. According to the designer, they are at once a little liberal and a little conservative in their tastes, and he has consequently given them a house that is both modern and traditional.

The house is similar in several respects to Seike's previous House for a Dancing Teacher (*Contemporary Japanese Houses*, Vol. I, pp. 23–34). It has, for example, the same large gabled roof with free-standing ridge-support pole at one end (§21). This device, which harks back to the most ancient Shinto shrine architecture, has fascinated Seike for a number of years. Another link between this house and the earlier one is the use of a low section resembling the traditional *doma* (§22 & COLOR §4), a ground-level kitchen and utility space found in farmhouses throughout Japan and much admired by many modern architects. In this house, the section in question is paved with black tile rather than with granite, as in the earlier house, and it contains only the dining room, rather than a dining-kitchen, but it is like the previous example in that it furnishes a central focal point for the whole building and is connected more or less directly with all the other principal rooms (§§22 & 26). As before, it contains the main stairway and is open to the ceiling of the second floor, so that warm air from its panel-heating system can flow into the second-story rooms. An innovation in the new building is an attractive balcony-hallway at the second-floor level (§23).

The living room, whose floor level is nearly a foot higher than that of the dining room, has a large picture window looking out over the fields to the south (§24). To the east of the living room are two small tatami rooms, one of which serves occasionally as a dining room for Japanese-style feasts (§25).

The master bedroom, which is on the south side, adjacent to the living room, is raised nearly four feet higher than the dining room and is therefore on middle ground between the first and second floors. It is approached from a landing on the main stairway. Two bedrooms on the second floor, which have projecting windows on the south, are used by the children. The house also has two large storage rooms inside and an additional concrete-block storage space next to the carport.

Despite the predominantly Japanese flavor, this building could easily be converted into a completely Western house. As it stands, it is an excellent solution to a number of problems that arise when it is necessary to have both Japanese-style and Western-style living spaces in a single building.

◁ *§19 A view from the north shows the rice fields and river on the south side of the house. Two second-story windows under the gable furnish light for the dining room (§§22 & 23; COLOR §4). In the foreground are tea bushes, green tea being the most famous product of the locality.*

◁ *§20 Behind the house are low mountains and a forest belonging to a Buddhist temple. The overall appearance of the house is reminiscent of Japanese farmhouse architecture of the past.*

§21 A close-up of the south side shows the picture window and free-standing ridge-support pole in the living room, as well as the projecting windows of the second-floor bedrooms. The small opening under the eaves at the left contains the windows of the master bedroom, which is on a level between the first and second floors. ▷

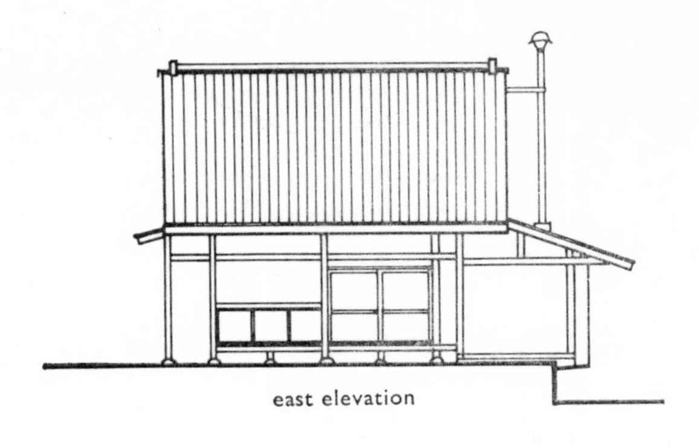

east elevation

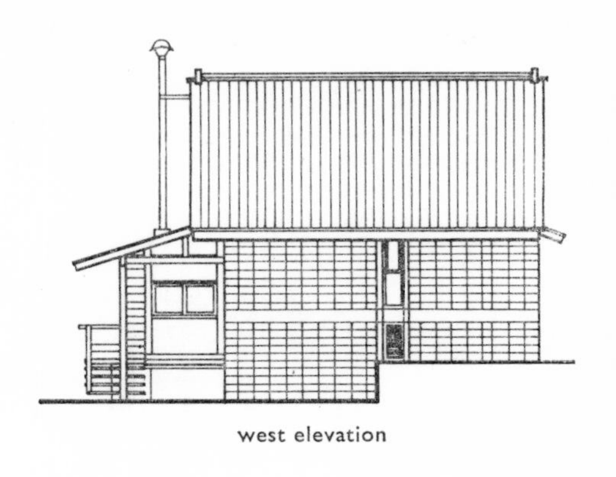

west elevation

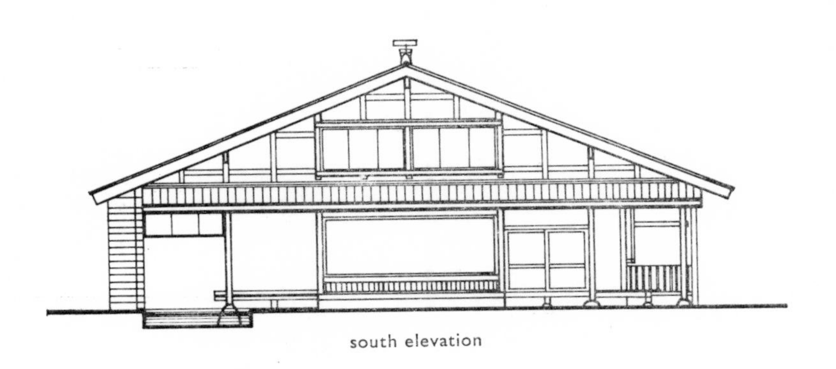

south elevation

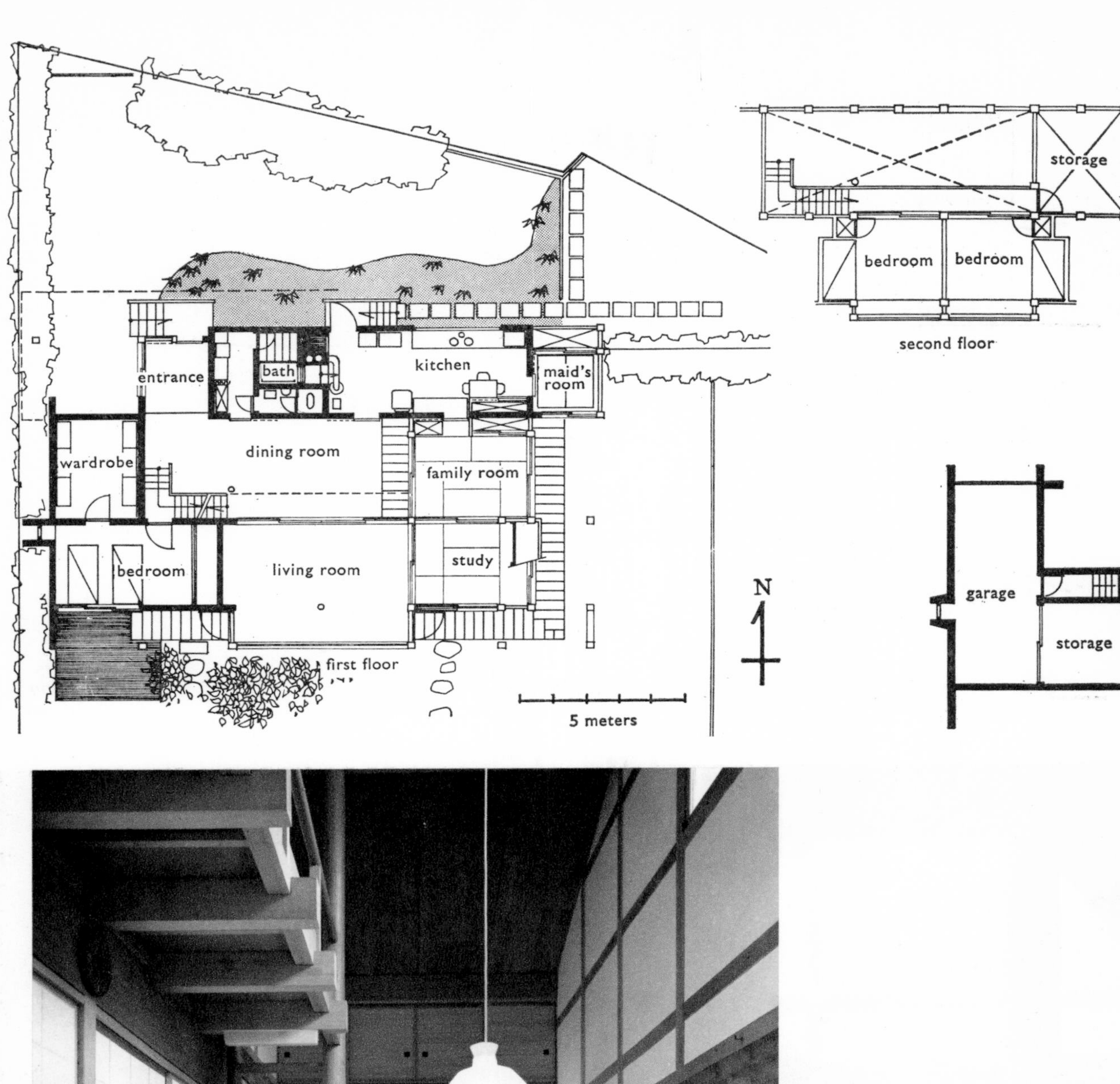

§22 The tile-floored dining room, open on the second-floor level, is the nucleus of the plan, and all other important spaces connect directly with it. The stairway at the far end of the room leads to the main bedroom, which opens on the landing at the turn, and to the balcony in front of the two second-floor bedrooms. The living room is to the left, behind the shoji, and the entrance, bathroom, and kitchen are to the right. The window partly visible at the extreme upper right is one of the pair mentioned in the note to §19.

COLOR §4 *A view of the dining room from the living room shows the white concrete-block wall of the kitchen and bath. The opening at the far left is the entrance hall. Panel heating is concealed under the black tile floor.*

§23 A view from the entrance hall shows the dining room, living room, and balcony. The sliding doors at the far end of the dining room open into a Japanese room, and the small door at the end of the balcony leads to a storage room.

§24 The large single-pane picture window in the living room looks out over the rice fields and river on the south.

§25 A tatami room at the southeast corner of the house, adjacent to the living room, serves as a study. Next to it is another tatami room, partly visible on the left, which is occasionally used as a substitute dining room. ▷

§26 When all the sliding panels on the first floor are removed, the living room, dining room, and two tatami rooms form one large, varied space that would make an excellent place for a party.

ONE-ROOM HOUSE

Architect: Shin Takaya
Location: Setagaya, Tokyo
Builders: Tōsei Construction Co.
Site area: 2,574 square feet
Building area: 716 square feet
Total floor area: 736 square feet
Estimated cost: $6,220.00

ALTHOUGH IT is the general practice in the smaller Japanese houses to use tatami-floored areas as all-purpose spaces, it is nevertheless customary to partition them into 3-mat, 4½-mat, 6-mat, or 8-mat rooms so that they can be shut off one from the other when necessary. The result is all too often an atomization of the house into a cluster of cubicles, which, even when combined by the removal of sliding doors, seem small and confining.

The designer of this little suburban house believes that the nature of interior space varies with the time of day and the needs of the moment, and that psychological partitions can often be as effective as physical ones, without actually breaking an interior into tiny pieces. To prove the point, he has experimented several times with small houses in which there is essentially only one room, large enough to provide a sense of spatial freedom, but at the same time organized into distinct areas whose functions vary with the hour and with the uses of the persons present.

In this house two distinct areas are set off by strips of *keyaki* (*zelkova acumenata*) flooring (best seen in COLOR §5 *and the plan*). One area contains a pit-with-table that can serve as a dining room, a study, or a sitting room, as the occasion demands (§28). The other serves as a bedroom at night and as almost anything else at other times. The main advantage of the design is simply that the occupants can feel at all times that they are in a spacious room, and hence a spacious house, even though the building is quite small. In good weather, doors on the south side can be drawn back into the casings on either side of a large opening (§31) to reveal a terrace that serves as an extension of the interior space (§32).

The house is owned by an architecturally aware couple who only half in jest point out that the one-room arrangement is conducive to marital bliss, if only because it makes the thought of serious quarrels almost unthinkable: there is no place to get off and sulk.

In the physical design of the building, there is a good deal that is reminiscent of traditional Japanese houses, but the throwing together of public and private spaces is profoundly un-Japanese, as is the implication that whoever comes as a guest is to be entertained by both husband and wife. The usual custom in Japan is for the husband to act as host while his wife remains unseen in a back room, appearing only occasionally to serve food and drink.

The only parts of the house not encompassed in the main room are a small kitchen and bath on the first floor and an attic room on the north side of the house for the owner's son (§33).

The omission of furniture is part and parcel of the designer's one-room idea, because furniture reduces or destroys the flexibility of the space. As long as it is a question of cushions or removable bedding, the "bedroom" space can be a sitting room or a sewing room or a tearoom, but put so much as a chest of drawers in it, and it becomes a bedroom, period. This line of thought is the functional reason for the large screen painting, which serves the necessary purpose of concealing the closets needed for clothing, bedding, and the like, and thus prevents these from determining the character of a large portion of the space.

◁ COLOR §5 *The color scheme, if indeed it can be called a "scheme," is furnished largely by the materials: light-colored Japanese cypress for the ceiling, posts, and woodwork; slightly darker* keyaki *for the table and wooden parts of the floor; off-white tatami and pure-white shoji. Accents are added by black cloth-covered walls and a striking geometric, abstract screen painting by Setsu Asakura.*

§27 Light from clerestory windows under the gables at either end of the room is softened by shoji. The cabinets at the left are for books.

§28 The northern half of the room is the eating and study area, whose pit-table is an elaboration of the traditional hori-gotatsu, *a square sunken hearth. A covered heater under the table furnishes warmth in the winter. The lighter shoji panel at the far end of the room is the main entrance. The other shoji link the room with the section containing the bath, kitchen, and child's room.*

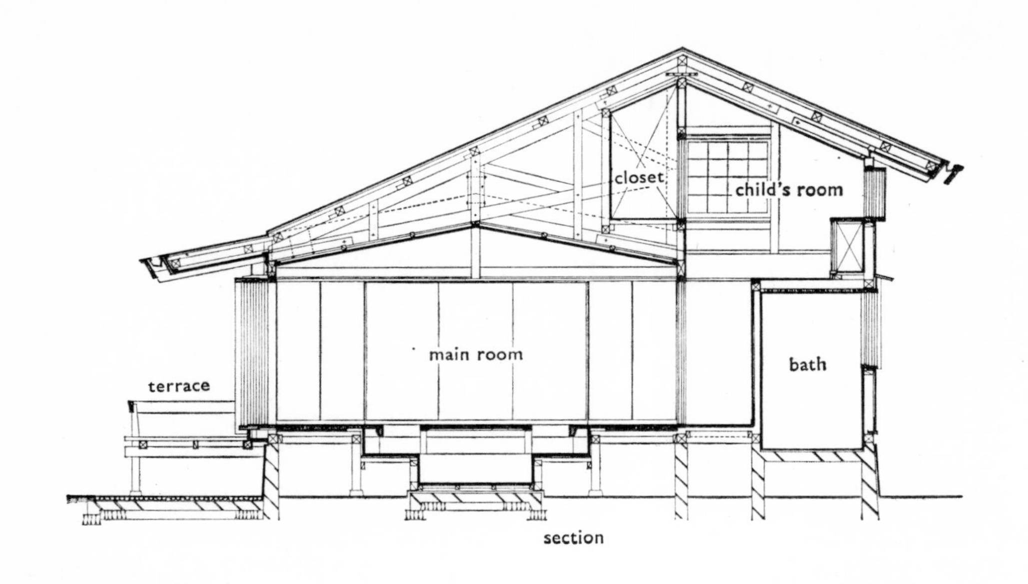

section

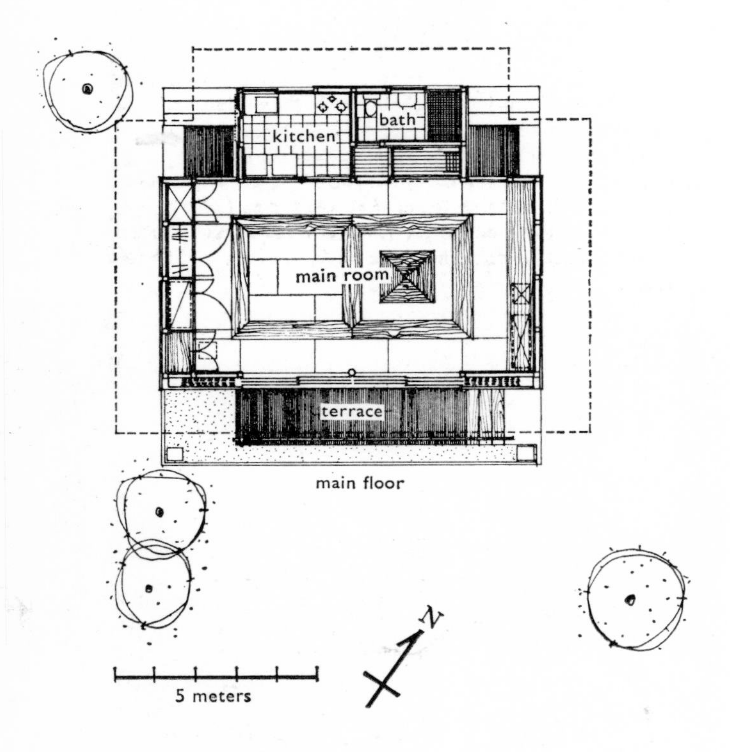

main floor

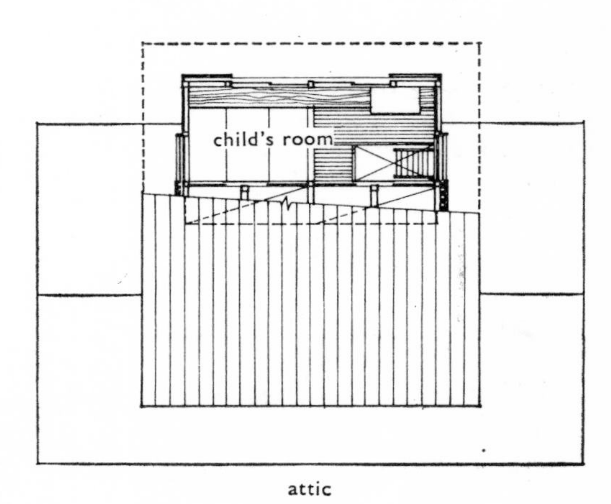

attic

§29 The large screen painting partially hides a series of closets that lines the west end of the house. The shoji at the left are of a type known as yukimi-shoji, which means that their lower halves are fitted with glass panels over which shoji can be raised or lowered.

§30 Visible at the lower center of the photograph is one of the large casings on either side of the opening that make it possible to slide the doors and screens back entirely out of view. The inverted V-shaped ceiling is known in Japanese as a funazoko-tenjō, *or "boat-keel ceiling."*

§31 The large opening and terrace run more than half the length of the south side of the house, giving light and a view of a tiny garden. The Japanese-cypress ceiling of the interior continues unbroken to the outer end of the eaves.

§32 Long eaves provide partial shelter for the terrace, which is floored with thick Japanese-cypress slats and has a simple, but stylish wooden railing.

§33 A small attic room has been fitted in under the eaves on the north side for the owner's teen-age son. Access is by means of a ladder.

IN THE OLD TRADITION

Architect: Seiichi Shirai
Location: Kureha, Toyama Prefecture
Builder: Ryōshun Tamura
Site area: 47,638 square feet
Total floor area: 2,944 square feet
Main house: 1,635 square feet
Estimated cost: $45,560.00

THE OWNER, a collector of Oriental art, is not only a man of traditional tastes, but fortunately one who was able to provide the architect with a large and beautiful site of the sort best suited to traditional Japanese houses. In addition to a splendid lawn and an abundance of trees, there is a panoramic view of mountains to the west and southeast and the Sea of Japan to the north.

The compound consists of a gatehouse (§§34 & 35), a main house (COLOR §6 & §37), and a separate library (§39). The three differ somewhat in feeling, but are linked by their series of low gabled roofs, their extended eaves, and the similar materials used for their structures and walls. An unusual feature of the design is that the owner and the architect chose chestnut wood for all wooden portions throughout the buildings. Even the frames of the shoji are of chestnut.

The gatehouse is, in effect, an elegant garage, from which extends a wall comprising a gateway. Both the garage and the gate are covered with gabled roofs made of wooden shingles and supported by heavy rafters that have been rounded on the bottom side to add mass (§§34 & 35). The ground shaded by the eaves is covered with gravel to form a sheltered walk, along the edge of which runs a shallow drainage ditch, lined and filled with rocks, for rainwater falling from the roof. This device, which has been used in Japan for centuries, is to be found in several of the other houses in this book.

A governing factor in the design of the main house was the need to provide a semi-private apartment for the owner's mother. In the plan, this is the two-room area to the left of the entrance, which has its own toilet and is provided by the hallway with easy access to the kitchen. One has the feeling that the living room, which even by Japanese standards is a little small for a house of this size, was sacrificed to some extent to make more room for the mother's Japanese-style living area. The house, however, is made up predominantly of Japanese rooms, and it seems likely that the 10-mat room described in the diagrams as a "guest room" is, from the functional viewpoint, the real living room.

The location is in snow country, and it was anticipated that the roof might have to bear the weight of as much as three feet of snow. Consequently, the supporting posts are unusually fat, and the longitudinal walls of the main house, while appearing to be ordinary *shinkabe* (that is to say, panels fitted in between posts, leaving the posts exposed), are in reality double walls. This arrangement, it should be pointed out, makes it possible for all outside door and window panels to be slid entirely out of view in the intervals between inner and outer walls (§38).

The library is essentially a private retreat and study for the owner, but its large tile-floored main room can, if necessary, accommodate a number of visitors, and a raised tatami platform at one end of this room furnishes a place for the tea ceremony, replete with a stone hearth for boiling water (§40).

◁ COLOR §6 *Long eaves cast a deep shadow over the clay walls of the main house, which were made in part of soil excavated when a well was dug on the site. In the distance to the right is the library.*

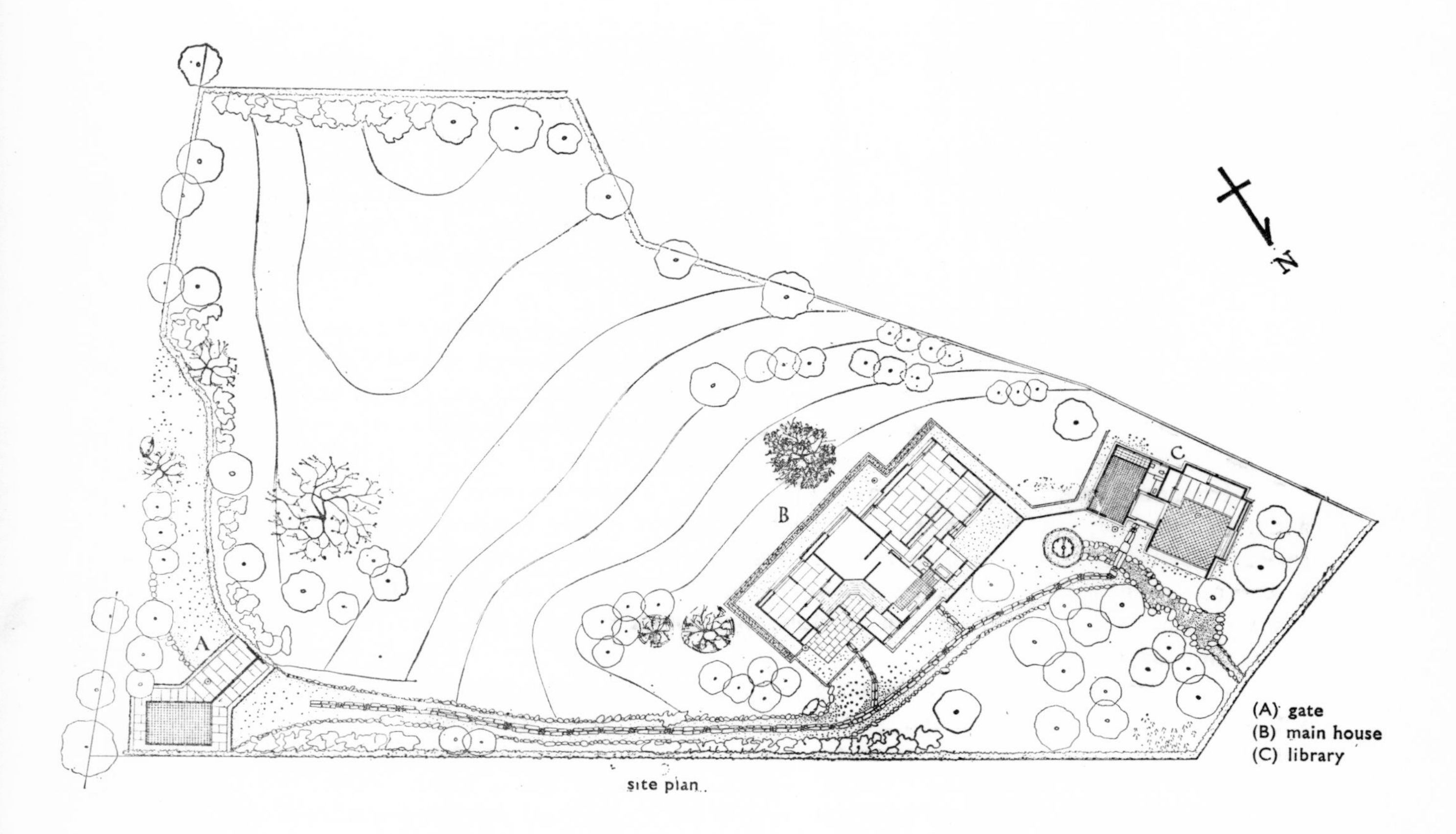

site plan

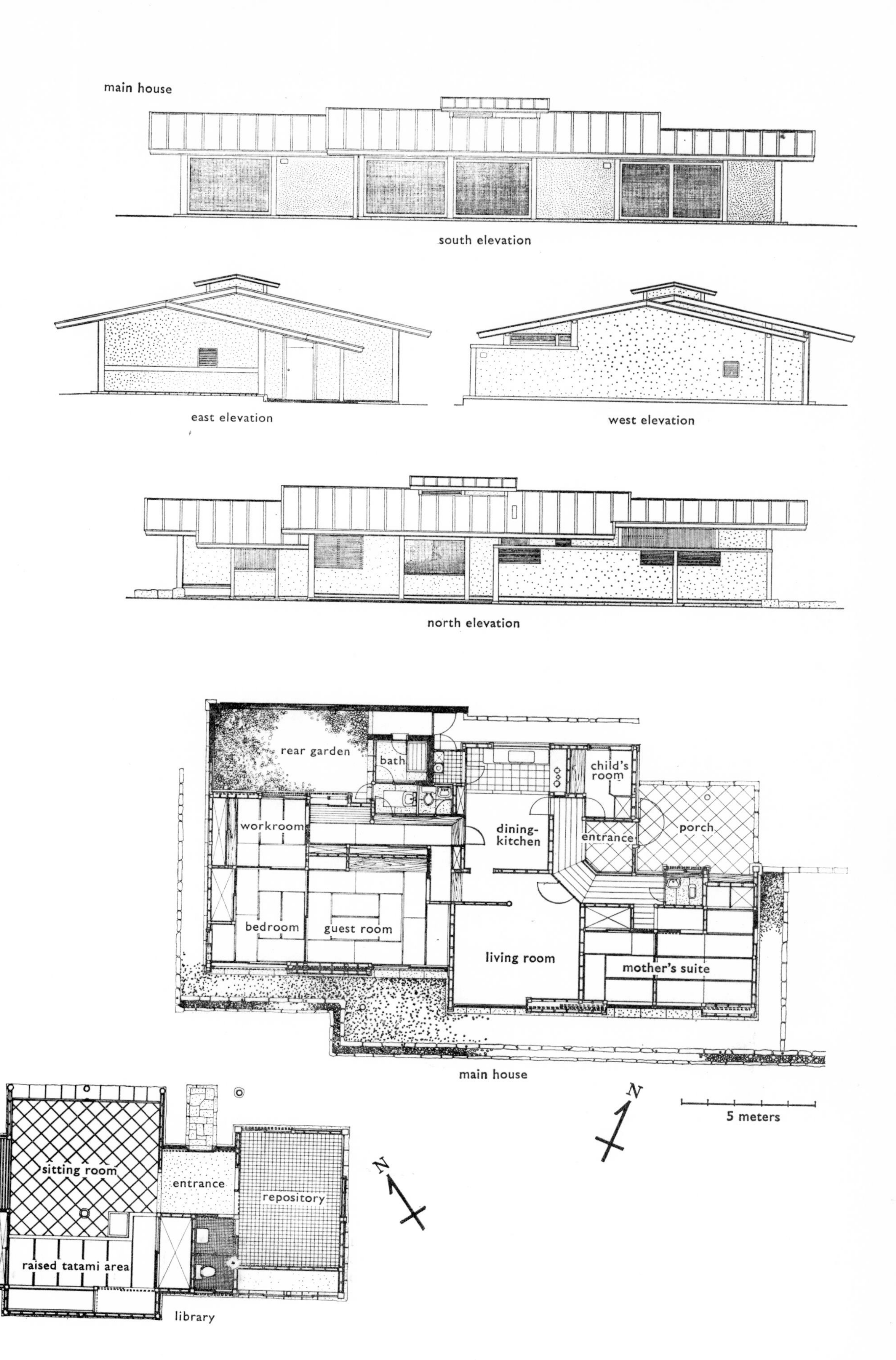
main house
south elevation
east elevation
west elevation
north elevation
rear garden
bath
child's room
workroom
dining-kitchen
entrance
porch
bedroom
guest room
living room
mother's suite
main house
N
5 meters
sitting room
entrance
repository
raised tatami area
library
N

§34 The main entrance to the compound is the gate at the extreme left. The gable that covers the gate connects at an oblique angle with the roof of the garage (right). The roof is shingled, and large semi-rounded rafters add heaviness and importance, as well as a certain rusticity.

§35 The gate and garage are surrounded by a gravel walk, which is sheltered by the eaves. Along the outer edge of the walk runs a rock-lined, rock-filled gutter that drains off water falling from the eaves—an ancient Japanese device. ▷

§36 The entranceway, which is paved with local stone, is sheltered by the long overhang of the roof. The grille at the left covers the window of the lavatory.

§37 The lines of the main house, whose south side is shown here, are gentle and direct. The main roof, which is of ribbed copper sheet, is broken near the middle by a small raised gable of a kind often used to ventilate the upper parts of Japanese farmhouses. All doors retract entirely into the casings behind the exterior walls.

§38 A night view shows the simply furnished living room on the right and the Japanese-style guest room on the left. Outer doors have been pulled fully back into their casings, leaving unobstructed openings each about ten feet wide.

§39 The library, which is similar in style to the main house, but has a uniform roof, serves not only as a private "den" for the owner, but as a storehouse for his collection of Oriental art objects. On the whole, its interior is less formal and more rustic than that of the main house.

§40 Inside the library, a heavy hexagonal post stands at the boundary between a large sitting room with a tiled floor and a raised section floored with tatami. The open stone hearth is for heating water to be used in tea ceremonies.

HOUSE ON THE BLUFF

Architects: Tatsuya Hirobe and Tadashi Okamura
Location: The Bluff, Yokohama
Builders: Iwamoto Construction Co.
Site area: 12,286 square feet
Building area: 1,977 square feet
Total floor area: 2,418 square feet
Estimated cost: $33,330.00

IN YOKOHAMA, the Bluff, a hilly area southwest of the business center, has for decades been considered the city's best residential district. Much of it has long since been preempted by the port's large foreign community, and its so-called "Foreigners' Cemetery" is a landmark, but the area also has many Japanese residents, among whom are the owners of this house.

The site, which is near the top of a hill, slopes down from south to north and affords a full view of the harbor on the northeast. Such topology is considered unfortunate in Japan, where for centuries people have felt that both the garden and the view should be on the warmer southern side of the house. Unwilling to sacrifice either the view or the garden on the south, the architect devised a compromise plan in which the main living rooms have the garden, but the second-floor suite, which is occupied by the owner's son and his wife, have the view. Making use of the natural slope, he worked out a split-level arrangement in which each of the three main sectors of the interior is separated from the others by a difference in height, but not so great a difference as to give one the impression of going upstairs or downstairs as one goes from one sector to another.

The entrance garden (§42) is at ground level on the northwest, or lowest, side of the property. A few steps lead up to a tiled porch at the south end of which is a large entrance hall. From here a short stairway leads up to the main living section (§§44 & 46) on the south, and another down to a ground-level wing on the northeast side, which contains a tearoom, its anteroom, and a maid's room (§47). The tearoom, which is large for its genre and can double as a guest bedroom, has a charming little garden of its own, set off from the main garden by a difference in ground level.

The living room, dining room, and kitchen, which have the same floor level, all face on the well-landscaped garden to the south (§43). A transition between house and garden is furnished by a large tiled veranda at ground level (COLOR §7 & §45), which is, for the most part, covered by a long extension of the roof. The treatment of the ceilings in this area is entertaining. The relatively low ceiling of the hallway emerges into the living room, where it covers a built-in sofa, but is then cut back to a higher level. At the boundary between the living room and the dining room, which are otherwise not partitioned, there is a second cutback, and on the veranda, a third. The ceiling thus gradually rises from a relatively low level in the stairway-hall to a plane flush with the lower edge of the eaves, each rise in level marking a functional transition.

On the east side of the living room and at a slightly higher level is a large tatami room (visible at right in §44) that serves as the master bedroom. This has its own veranda, set at the same level and floored with wood. A pleasant touch is added at the outer rim of the porch by a number of box gardens set into the floor.

From the hallway approaching the living room, a short flight of stairs leads up on the west side of the building to the second-floor bedroom (§48), which has its own small kitchen and dining nook (§49). In the bedroom the ceiling follows the lines of the central peak of the roof, and there is a large clerestory window under the "gable."

The occupants of the house, when asked their opinion of it, expressed particular satisfaction both with the degree of privacy achieved in the three main sections and, somewhat paradoxically, with the ease of movement from one level to another.

◁ *§41 As seen from the street, the house rises to a dramatic three-pronged peak, affording an excellent view of the harbor from the second-story windows. Lower parts of the house are mostly of concrete, scraped and finished with stucco; upper parts, which include the main living quarters, are of wood.*

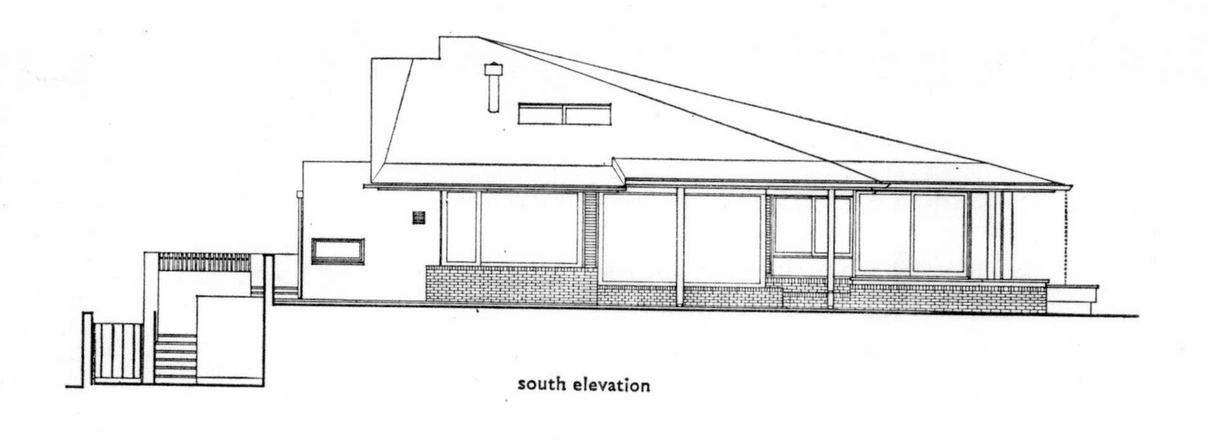

south elevation

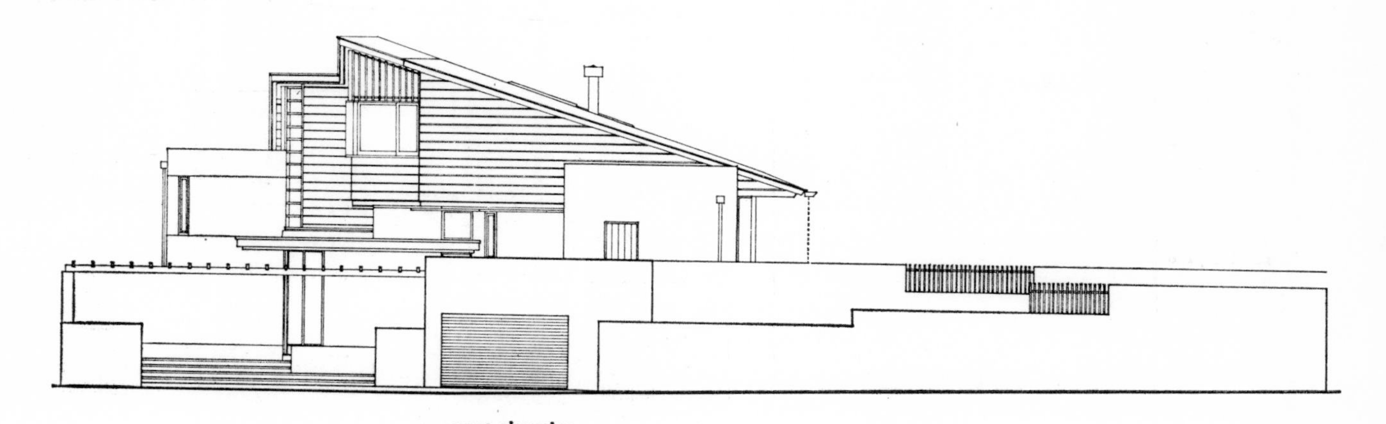

west elevation

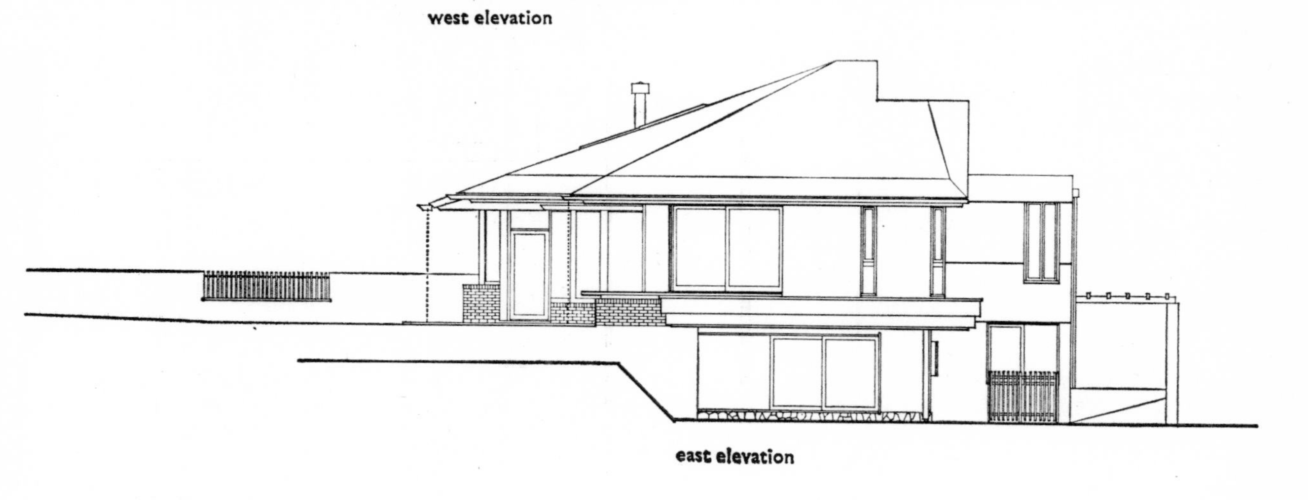

east elevation

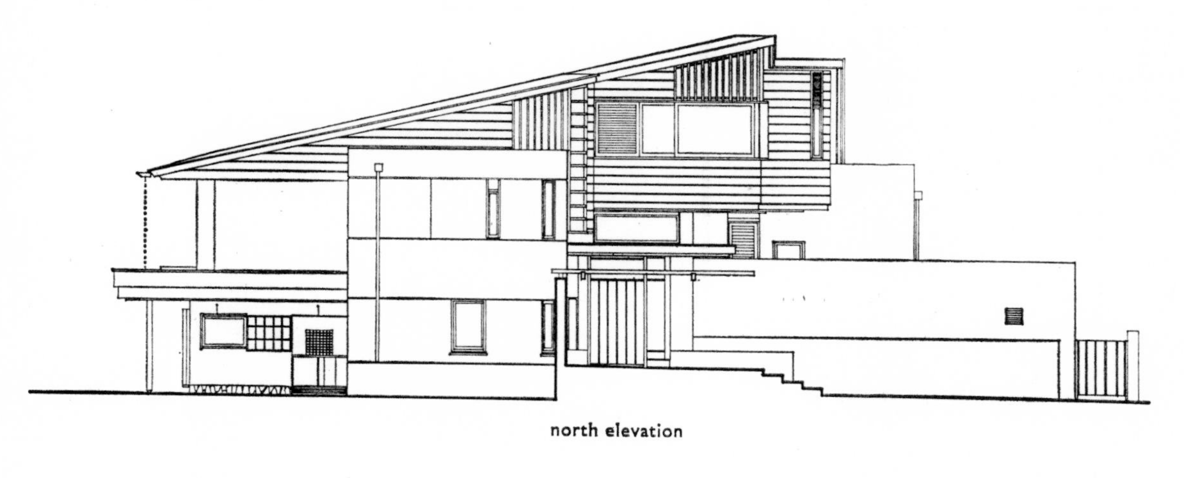

north elevation

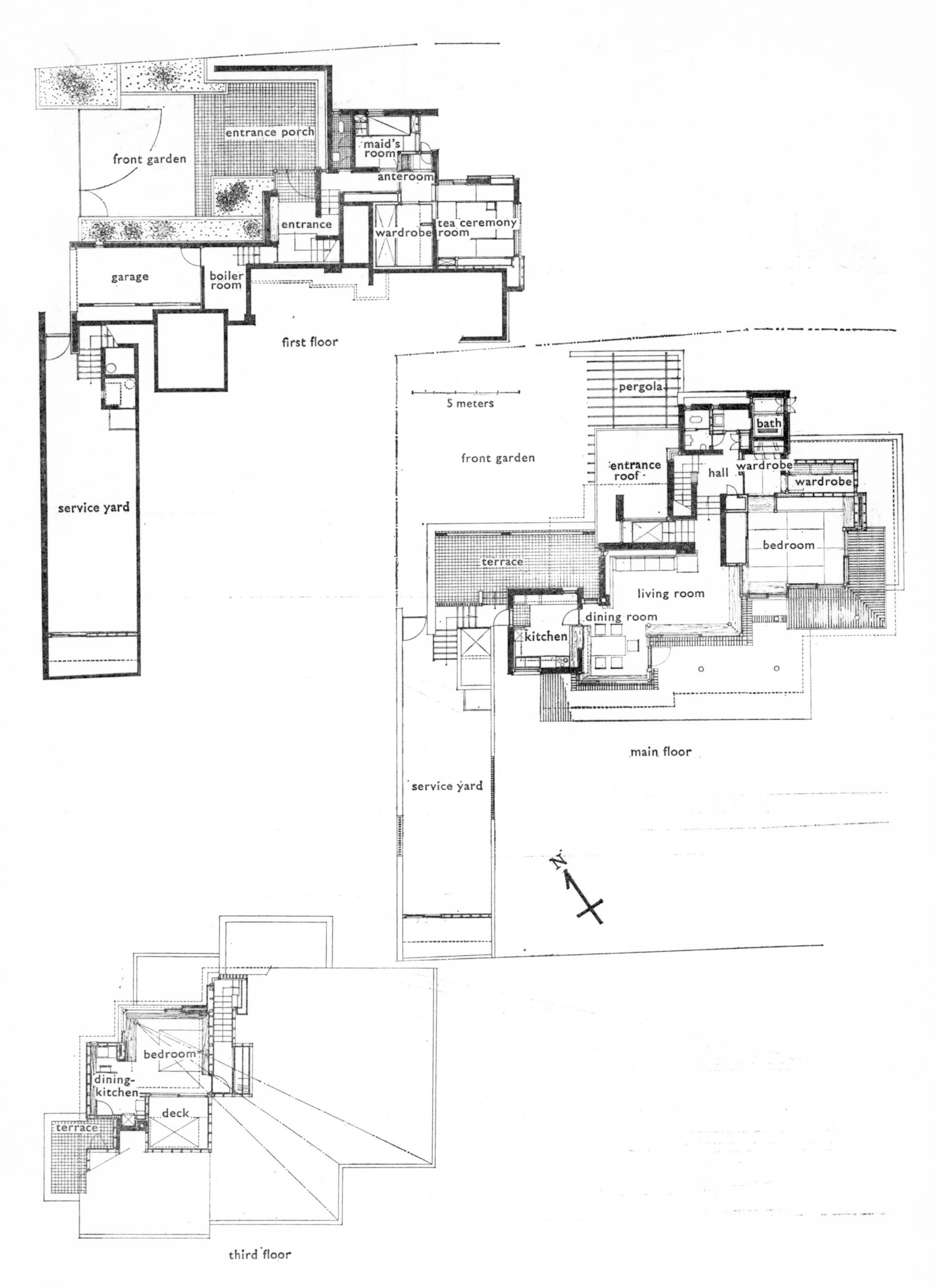
front garden
entrance porch
maid's room
anteroom
entrance
wardrobe
tea ceremony room
garage
boiler room
first floor
service yard
pergola
5 meters
bath
front garden
entrance roof
hall
wardrobe
wardrobe
bedroom
terrace
living room
dining room
kitchen
main floor
service yard
N
bedroom
dining-kitchen
deck
terrace
third floor

§42 The broad entranceway, with its natural stone, plants, concrete and wooden walls, and play of light and shadow, has a distinctly Wrightian look. The front door is at the right end of the tiled porch.

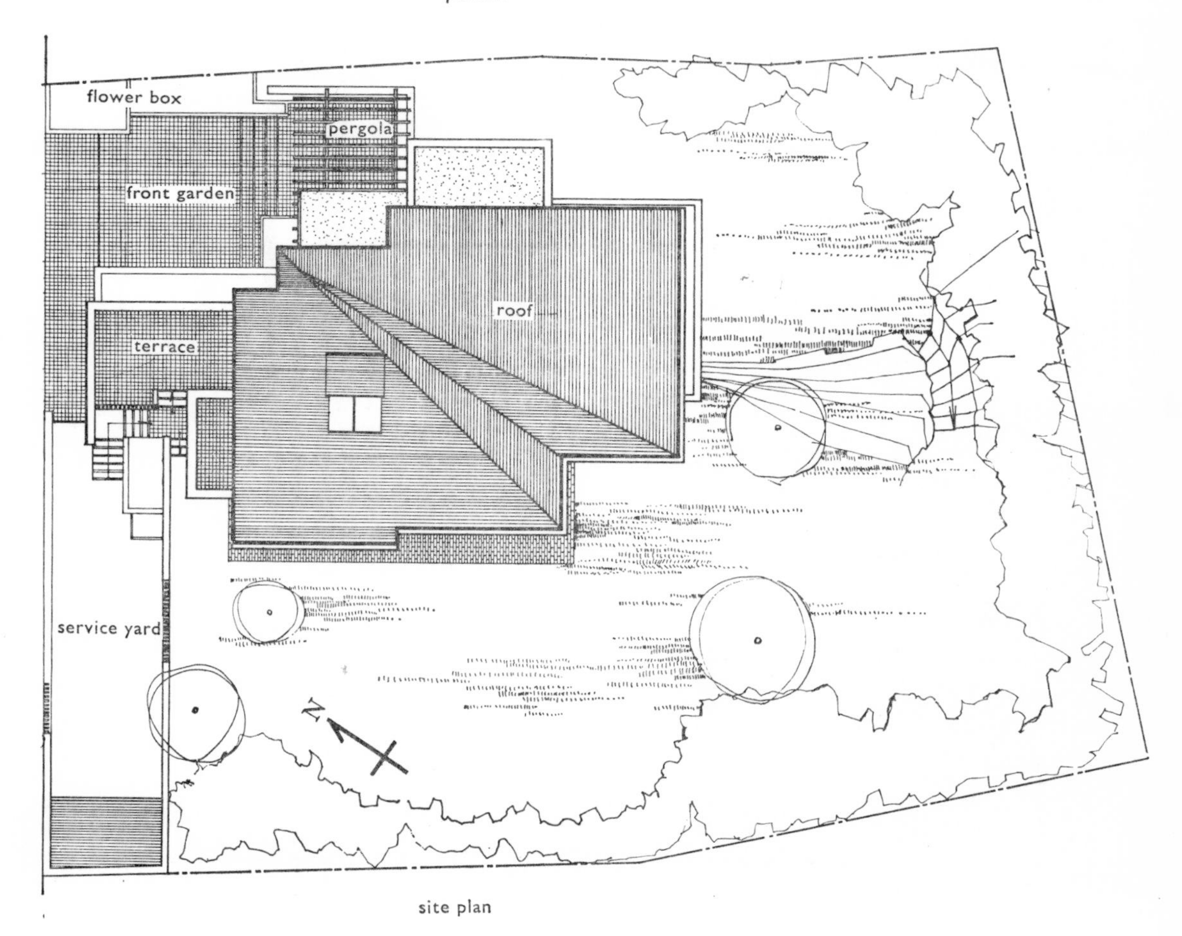

site plan

§43 On the south side, the terrace furnishes a transition between house and garden. The rooms from left to right are the kitchen (stucco wall), dining room, living room, and, at a higher level, master bedroom.

§44 A night view from the south shows the dining room, the living room, and the shoji of the master bedroom.

COLOR §7 *The glossy red tiles of the covered terrace furnish a bright contrast to the neutral tones of the house and the abundant greenery of the well-kept garden. The raised porch in the distance is adjacent to the master bedroom.*

◁ §45 *The ceilings of the porches are of spruce, stained and varnished, as are the ceilings of the living and dining rooms. The rope hanging from the eaves at the center of the photograph guides falling rainwater from the roof gutters to a rock-filled drainageway below.*

§46 The west and north walls of the living room are lined with shelves and built-in furnishings. The room is indirectly lit by fluorescent lamps above the ledge at the upper right.

§48 The ceiling of the upstairs bedroom follows the lines of the central peak of the roof. Ordinary windows provide a good view of Yokohama harbor, and a clerestory window with a grille furnishes additional light.

◁ §47 An 8-mat tearoom and its small anteroom form a suite for guests at the ground-floor level on the northeast side; that is to say, about half a floor below the entrance hall and nearly a full floor below the living room and dining room.

§49 Since the second floor is a semi-private apartment for the owner's son and his wife, it is furnished with a small kitchen and dining nook of its own.

TOWN DWELLING

Architect: Tadayoshi Fujiki
Location: Shinjuku, Tokyo
Builders: Itō Construction Co.
Site area: 947 square feet
Building area: 364 square feet
Total floor area: 1,092 square feet
Estimated cost: $10,000.00

JAPANESE CITIES in general sprawl rather than rise, and even in Tokyo the average height of buildings is only about 1.6 stories, despite the great spate of construction that has produced so many eight- and nine-story office buildings in the past ten years. The whole idea of building up instead of out is still comparatively new in Japan, and the concept of private houses with three or four floors is still strange to most people, for unlike London, Paris, or New York, Japanese cities have never gone through a phase of several-storied residences.

On the other hand, urban land prices are currently so high that the average white-collar worker is lucky if he is able to own as much as 2,000 square feet in the distant suburbs. In the Shinjuku district of Tokyo, the less than 1,000 square feet on which this house stands would, at the time of this writing, probably fetch the yen equivalent of thirty-five thousand United States dollars, and it would be a safe guess that the aggregate of urban land appearing in this book would be valued at something like three times the cost of the houses standing on it, even if the more expensive houses are included.

Such being the case, architects are beginning to experiment with three- and four-story residences that give the occupants an adequate floor area in a minimal building space. Because of the ever present danger of earthquakes, buildings of this height require rigid frames, and the most economical building material available is reinforced concrete. Unfortunately, reinforced concrete is not the world's friendliest material to the sight or touch, and unless it is concealed by expensive finishing, the average man is apt to consider it inappropriate for a house, not to say ugly.

In this house, which the architect—no average man—designed for himself and his family, the treatment of the concrete on the exterior is frankly brutal, but the use of wood for the balconies vastly reduces the severity of the facade (§§50 & 51), and the interior differs very little in feeling from many present-day Japanese wooden-frame houses (COLOR §8 & §53). On the roof, where the architect has made a grassy playground for his son, the sturdiness of the high concrete railing is welcome (§56).

The designer writes: "If you watch a child playing, you find that he hides in dark places and runs round and round in the house. He rarely sits still for a long time in open, well-lit spaces. His insatiable curiosity drives him to bump up against everything, and in this way he learns what life is about. We all like at times to go and lie in an open field, but at others we would prefer to climb a mountain. What we want today is not necessarily what we want tomorrow. It may seem contrary, but this is the way we like and demand to live, and when one designs a house, one must keep this important aspect of life in mind."

With this thought, the architect has tried to endow his house with maximum flexibility, using few partitions and avoiding an excess of the sort of furniture that tends to take root in one spot. Though there are basic fixed sections, such as the kitchen and the bath, the other rooms of the house are all-purpose, interchangeable spaces.

A convivial terrace on the ground floor (§52) provides a link with the outside and with the neighbors, and the relatively large porch on the second floor (§§54 & 55) serves as an outdoor living or dining room, as well as a substitute for a garden.

◁ *§50 Though the facade is somewhat forbidding, its frankness and practicality have an architectural appeal. Essentially this is a three-room house, with study-office on the first floor, living-dining room on the second, and bedroom on the third, with a gradual increase in privacy as one goes up.*

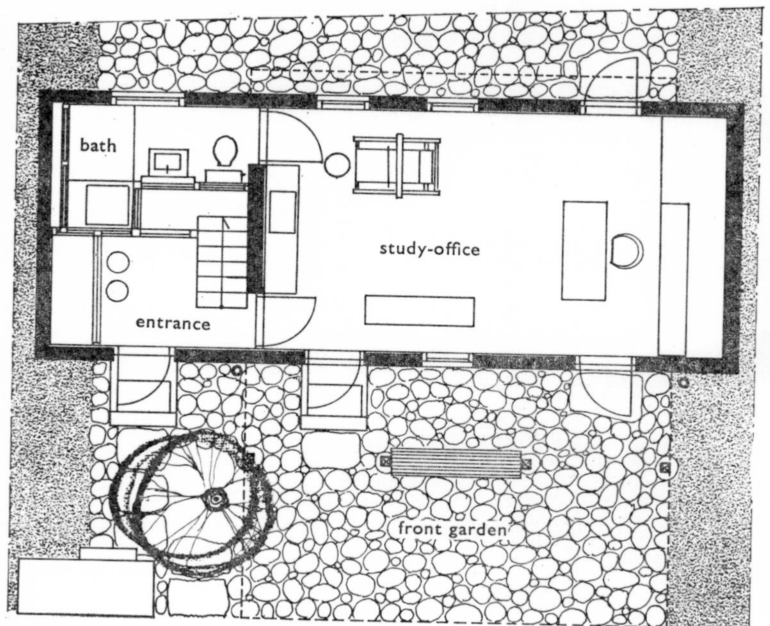

first floor

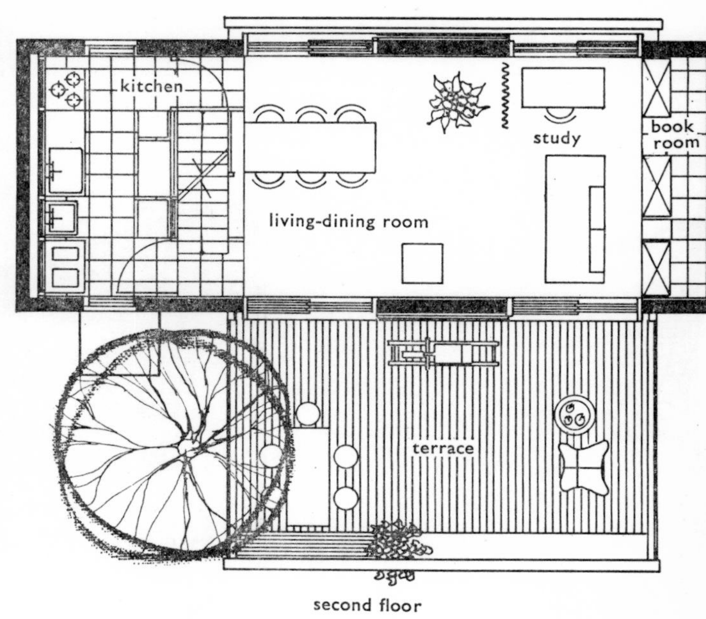

second floor

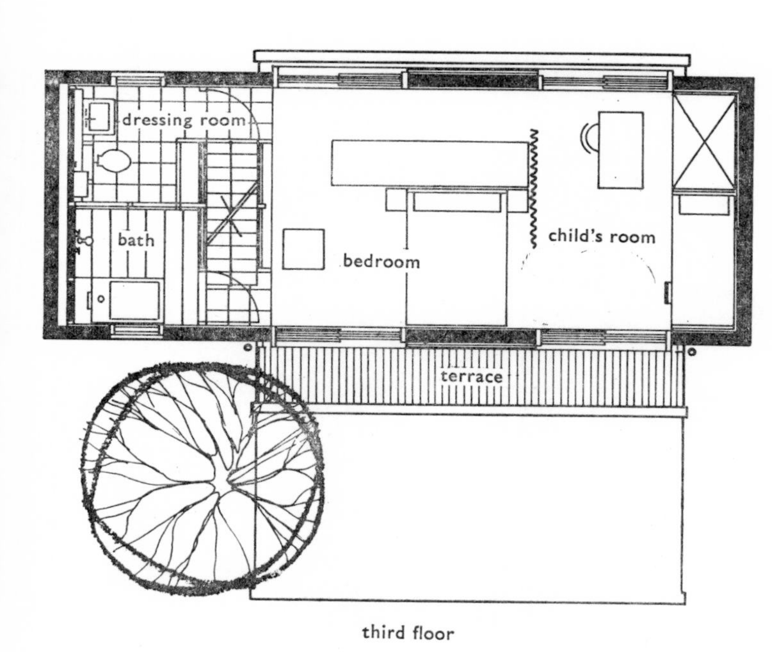

third floor

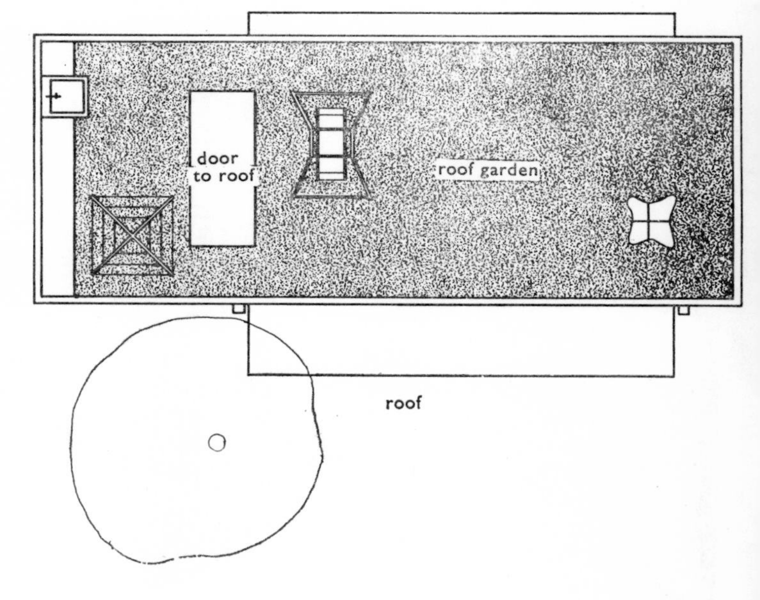

roof

N

5 meters

§52 The entrance porch is a halfway ground between the family within and the neighborhood without—a modern version of the sociable "front stoop" of crowded areas in New York.

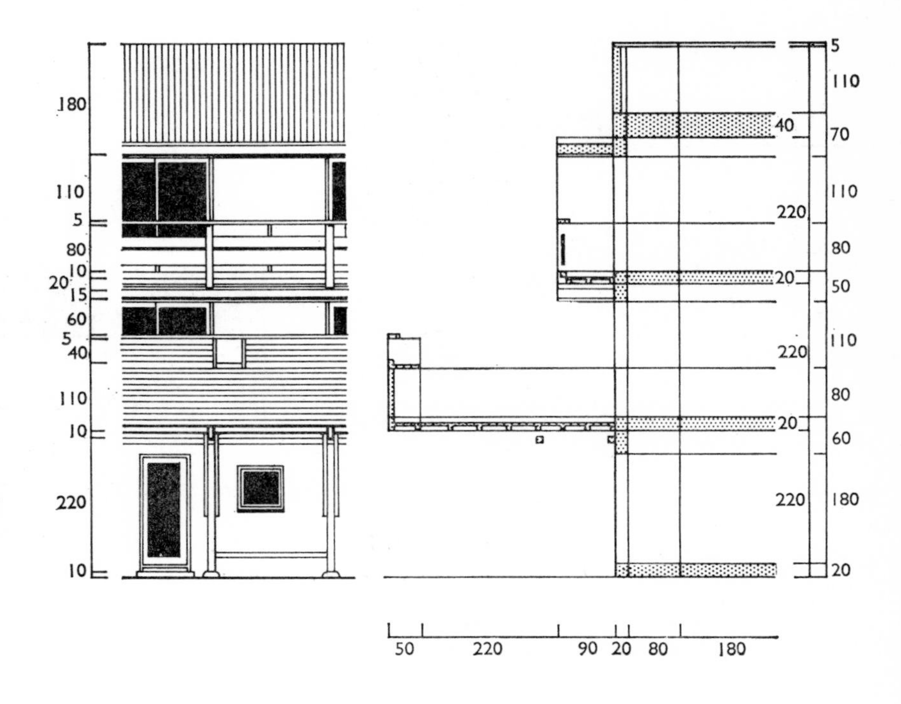

◁ *§51 The stone-paved entrance portico and the wooden balconies do much to lessen the severity of the concrete walls, and the second-floor balcony is an effective extension of the living area (see §§54 & 55).*

COLOR §8 *The interior decor plays down the concrete casing and is not, all in all, very different from what one would expect to find in a small, modern wooden-frame house in the suburbs of Tokyo or Osaka. Only the simplest furnishings and the most necessary partitions are used. The door to the right of the cabinet leads to the kitchen.*

§53 *The living-dining space on the second floor has, not one, but two doors opening onto its balcony, whose high, solid front wall largely conceals it from the street.*

§54 The balcony can be protected from the sun with awnings hung from hooks on the front wall and the third-floor balcony.

§55 A view of the second-floor balcony from above shows a small, but pleasant substitute for a garden, neither completely shut off from the city nor completely open to it.

§56 A grassy garden on the roof, surrounded by a solid-concrete fence, provides a safe and sunny playground for the owner's son and his friends, as well as a place where the grown-ups can sunbathe.

HOUSE FOR ACTORS

Architect: Kamon Tatehata
Location: Shiba, Tokyo
Builders: Shiraishi Construction Co.
Site area: 2,470 square feet
Building area: 919 square feet
Total floor area: 1,665 square feet
Estimated cost: $25,000.00

THE SHAPE of the lot was extremely irregular, and in order to secure a garden space on the south (§59), while still allowing parking space on the north (§§57 & 58), the designer devised a hexagonal plan that enabled him to fit the building well up into a triangular projection of the land on the north. As a result, none of the rooms is rectangular, but the designer turned the irregularity into an advantage by leaving a part of the living-dining area open to the second-floor ceiling (§61& COLOR §9) and creating in the central sector of the house a stairway and balcony (§§60 & 62) that provide a spatial nucleus for the house, as well as excellent lines of movement from room to room. The sides of the stairway, as well as the outer walls of the balcony, are parallel to the exterior walls.

The irregular house is covered by an equally irregular roof with two "folds." On the east side the roof slopes downward more drastically than on the west, and the relatively low second-floor space underneath it is used as a storage attic. All second-floor rooms open on the balcony, which doubles as a library.

Both the owner of this house and his wife are well-known actors, and since they do a good deal of entertaining, the public space in the house has been made comparatively large. Area aside, the high open space above the dining room gives a fine sense of spaciousness, and the balcony and winding stairway form an eminently appropriate setting for an "entrance" from the second floor. One can virtually see the owner's stylish wife waving from the balcony steps to guests below and then descending to greet them—a momentary pause at the turn near the bottom to smooth her dress for the last few important steps. It is an excellent set.

Whether by design or by accident, there is more than a little in this interior of Frank Lloyd Wright: witness the natural cypress or pine walls, the interesting overhangs, the flow of space, and the windows in odd corners. In general, Wright's direct influence on modern Japanese architecture has been surprisingly small. A few devoted men who worked with him on the Imperial Hotel in Tokyo have continued to design in a style reminiscent of that famous building (soon, unfortunately, to be destroyed), but by and large Wright's affection for Japan has not been returned. Curiously, however, in the past few years something approaching the Wrightian touch has been cropping up increasingly in the better-designed Japanese houses, even those designed by young architects who have no visible links with Wright or his Japanese disciples. Perhaps the simplest and best explanation is that good ideas have a way of catching on everywhere sooner or later.

◁ COLOR §9 *The space above the dining room is open, so that the gallery on the second floor looks down on the living-dining area. A lampshade of amber and greenish-brown beads adds sparkle to the quiet color scheme. This area, stairway included, forms a spatial nucleus around which the remainder of the house is gathered.*

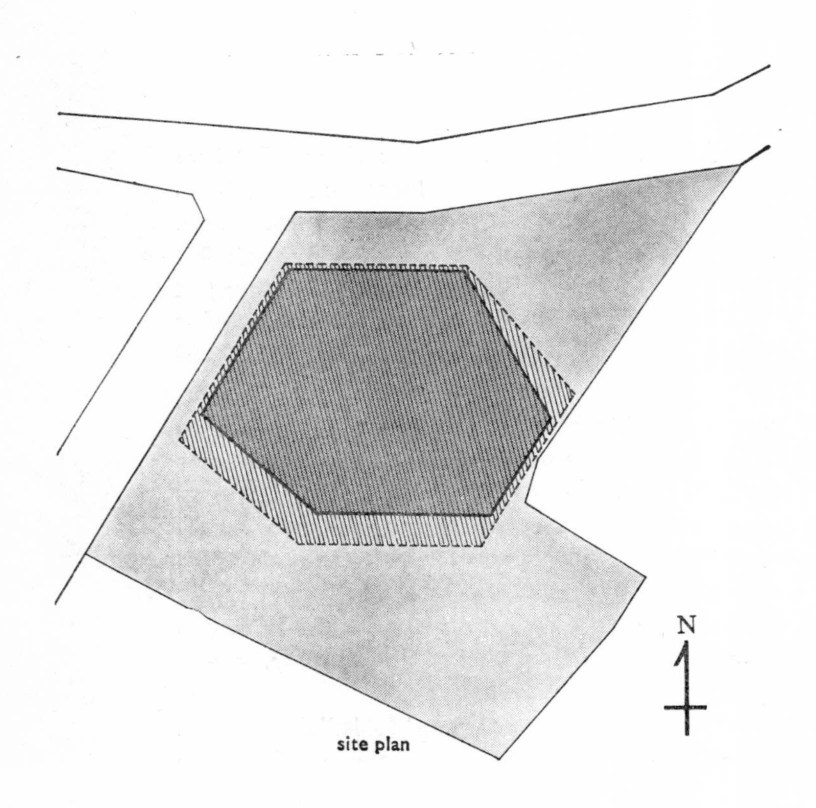

site plan

§57 A view from the second floor shows the driveway and front steps on the north. The curving pattern of the brick paving contrasts with the angular patterns of the house itself. ▷

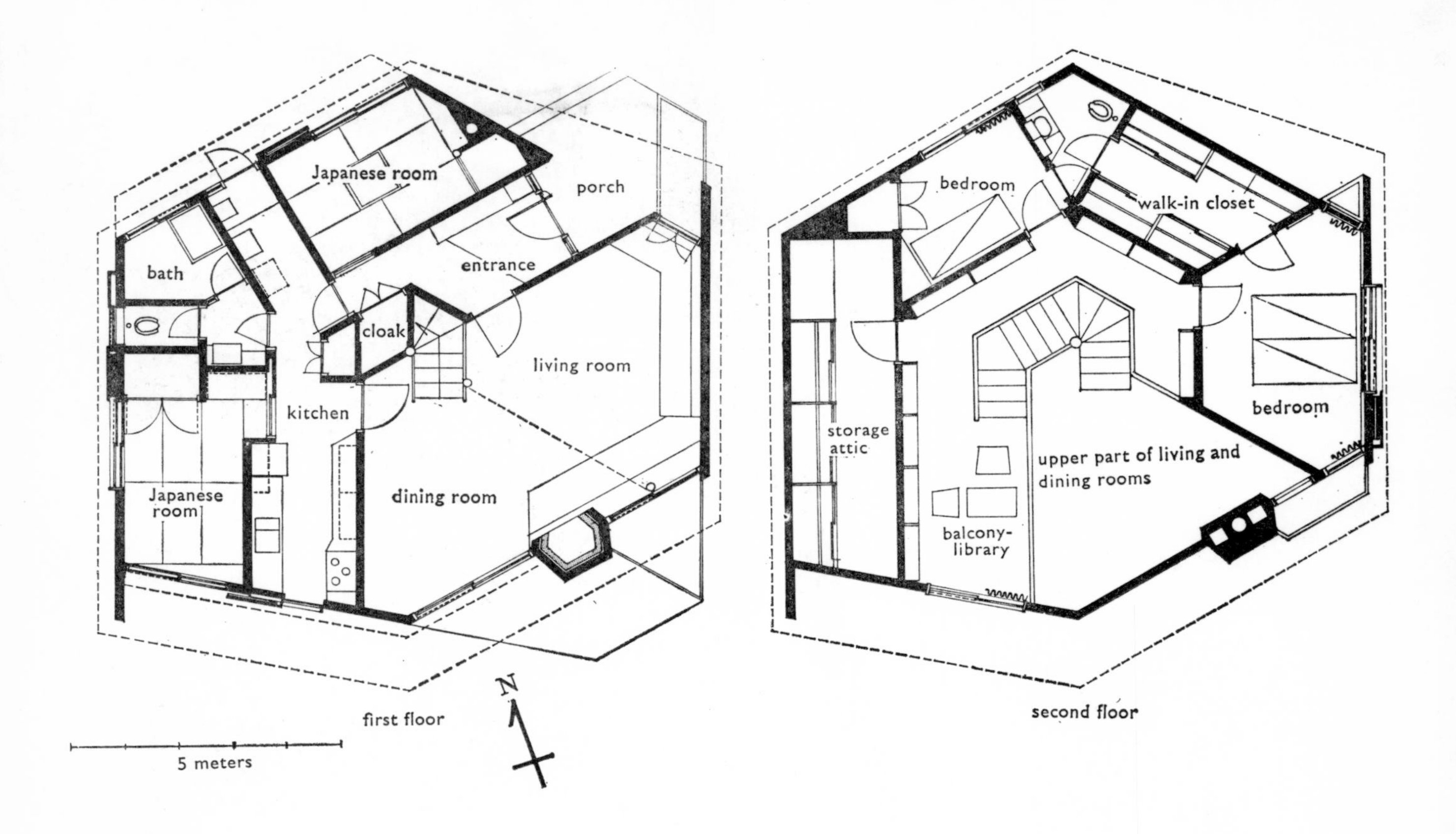

§58 A view from the entrance of the driveway on the north shows the front door and the small porch before it. The window at the left is in the corner of the living room.

§59 The hexagonal shape of the house permitted it to be fitted into a triangular protrusion of the lot on the north, thus leaving space for a small garden on the south, shown here. Inside, the rooms are all of irregular shape, and the oblique angles of the interior are repeated in the brick-paved terrace outside the dining room. The balcony at the upper right opens off one of the two second-floor bedrooms, but the patterned window to its left is in the clerestory of the living-dining room.

◁ *§60 The central stairway leads up from the dining room to the second-floor gallery. The walls in this area, as well as in the remainder of the living-dining room are of cypress boards, set vertically. The sides of the winding stairway are parallel with the exterior walls of the house.*

§61 A view from the balcony shows the fireplace, whose hearth extends to the left from a window seat. The space under the overhang at the upper left is the living room.

§62 The second-floor gallery is a combination of hallway, balcony, and library. The doors lead to the two bedrooms (right and center) and to the attic storage room under the lower eaves on the west side of the house.

HOUSE WITH A CLOSED FRONT

Architect: Junzō Yoshimura
Location: Gotanda, Tokyo
Builders: Harada Construction Co.
Site area: 4,680 square feet
Building area: 2,798 square feet
Estimated cost: $77,770.00

ALTHOUGH IT is estimated that about half of the eleven million residents of Tokyo now live in apartment houses, the apartment house is a relatively new institution in Japan, and the average Japanese man, even in this great congested city, longs for his own house and garden. To give him this in limited spaces and amid the noisy scramble of urban life, Japanese architects have tried a number of interesting solutions, of which this house represents one of the more outstanding.

The building is very close to the front of the lot on the west side, and, street noises being what they are, the architect chose to insulate the house on this side with what amounts to a solid concrete wall (§63). To avoid visual monotony, he decorated the surface of the wall with a simple geometrical design in low relief, but the house definitely presents a closed face to the street. By way of pleasant contrast, behind the wall one finds the delightful openness of traditional Japanese architecture. The house is placed near the north edge of the lot, and there is a well-landscaped garden on the south. The total effect of the plan is similar in many ways to that of an inner-court house.

From the entranceway, which is floored with marble (§64), it is possible for business guests to walk across an inner garden of gravel and bamboo (§65) to the owner's study, without entering the house proper. The study is, in effect, a descendant of the "receiving room," or *ōsetsu-ma*, a Western-style room, largely for formal use or simply for show, that became *de rigueur* in middle-class Japanese houses during the early days of Westernization. Though this room was often an anomaly in the earlier stages of its development, it can be, and in this house is, very useful as a place for dealing with people whom one does not wish to invite into the house proper.

Beyond the entrance hall and study are a large living room (COLOR §10) and a dining room (§66), both facing on a rectangular pond that separates the front section of the garden from the more private section in the back (§§67 & 69). A small open porch reminiscent of the traditional "moon-viewing platform" extends from the living room out over the pond.

It is characteristic of the designer, Junzō Yoshimura, and his associates that the garden is not only sensitively planned, but well integrated with the house. Except for the kitchen, behind which is a small back garden, every room in the house has a view of the main garden, and the mood outside so well matches the mood inside that each room on the lower floor seems indeed to have its own private landscape, ranging in style from the relatively formal area outside the study and living room to the informal area outside the family room (§68).

The upstairs bedrooms (§70) are provided with a balcony, at one end of which is a sun deck (§69), sheltered from the street by a lattice. In addition to small closets in each of the bedrooms, there is a large closet room at the west end of the second floor.

The house is heated and cooled by a three-zone air-conditioning system, with machinery in a small basement and controls in the kitchen.

◁ *§63 The house and garden are shut off from the street on the west side by a windowless concrete wall, but the monotony of a plain concrete surface has been avoided by the use of a geometric pattern in low relief. The main entrance is under the portico left of center. The door at the right leads to the garden.*

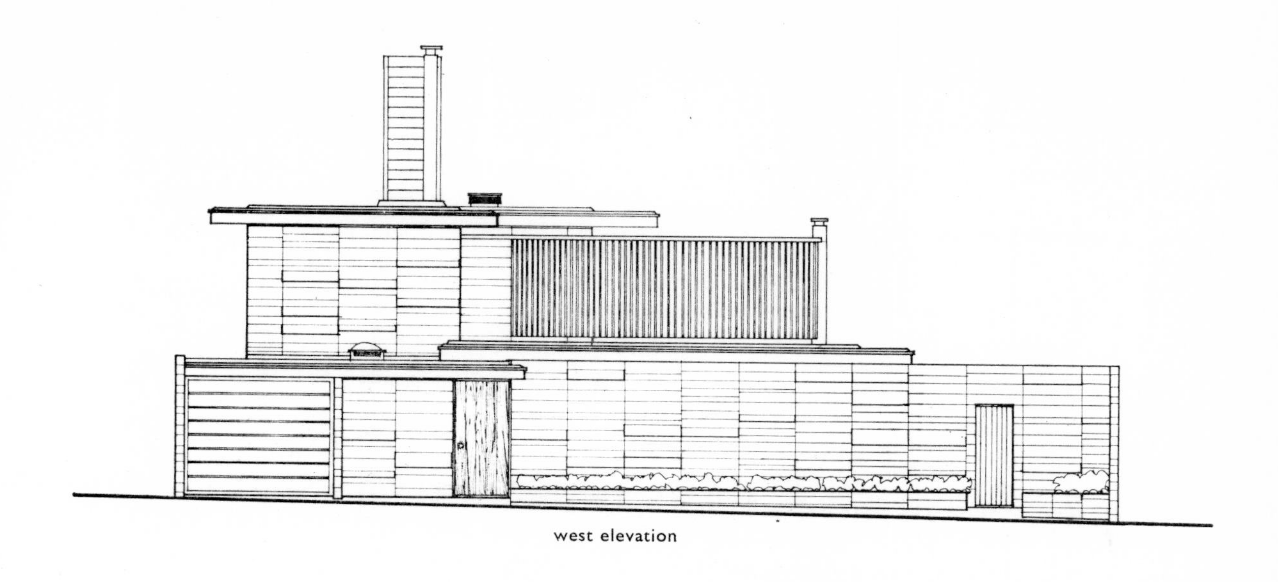

west elevation

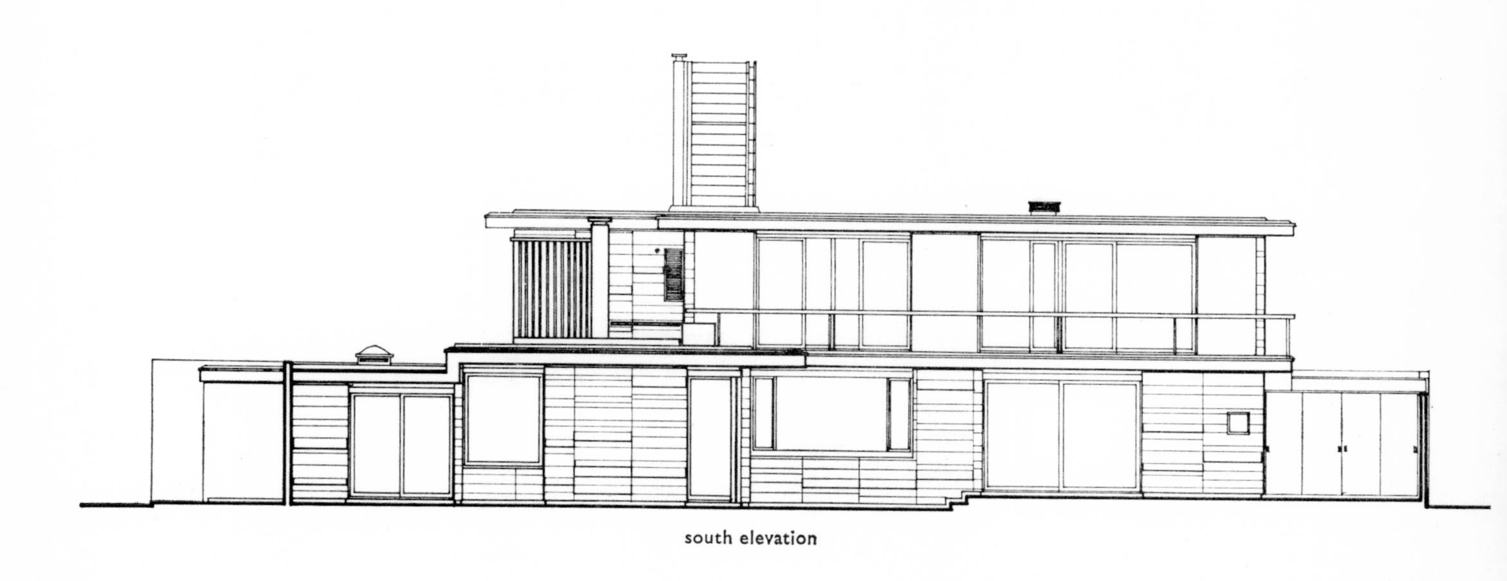

south elevation

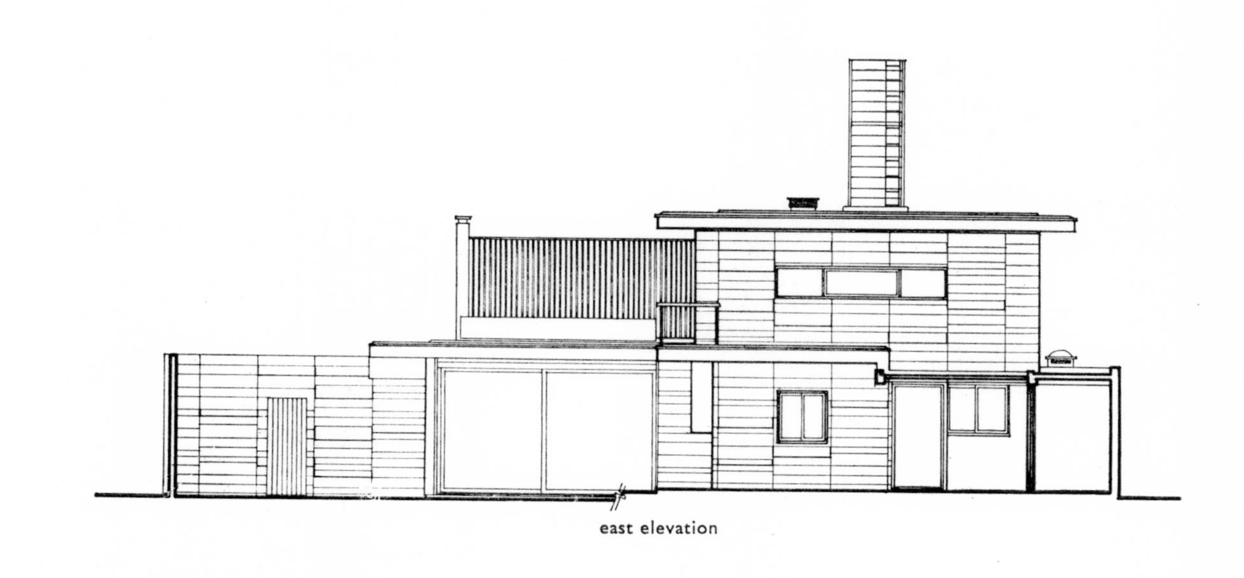

east elevation

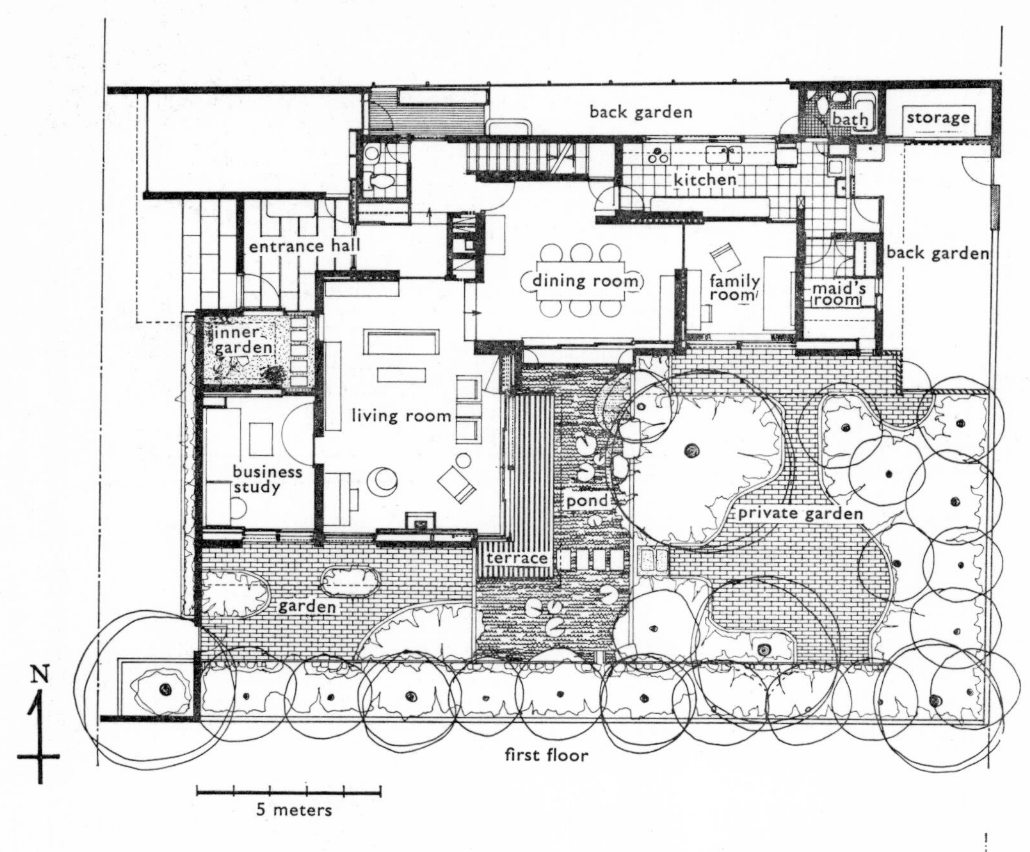
back garden
bath
storage
kitchen
entrance hall
dining room
family room
maid's room
back garden
inner garden
living room
business study
pond
private garden
terrace
garden
N
first floor
5 meters

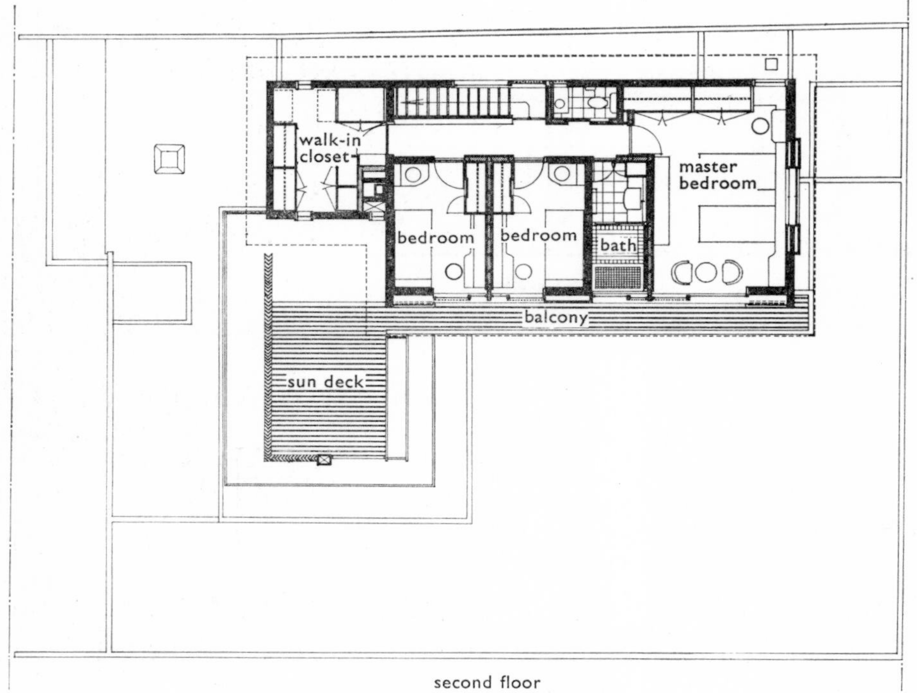
walk-in closet
master bedroom
bedroom
bedroom
bath
balcony
sun deck
second floor

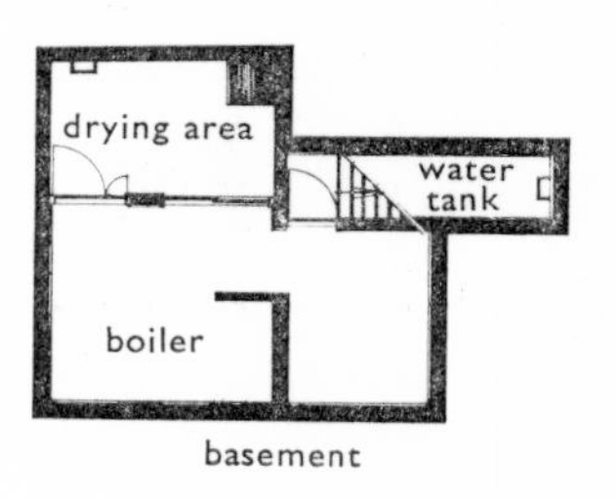
drying area
water tank
boiler
basement

§64 The spacious entrance hall has a marble floor, and, on the north side, a built-in bench. The round glass object by the umbrella stand is a float from a large fishing net. The light on the left comes from the adjacent inner garden (§65).

COLOR *§10 The spacious living room has large openings on the south (directly ahead) and east. Except for the fireplace, which is of painted concrete block, all the walls are of plaster. The ceiling is of lauan plywood. The open door on the right leads to the owner's study, and the large glass sliding doors on the left open on a terrace that projects over a small pond (§67).*

◁ *§65 The small inner garden next to the entrance offers direct access to the owner's study for business callers. The opening in the roof over the garden furnishes light for the entrance hall and, via the narrow window to the left of the first stepping stone, to an otherwise darkish corner of the living room.*

§66 The dining room, which is adjacent to the living room, also has white plaster walls and a lauan-plywood ceiling. On the right is a projecting window with an inside box garden. The window looks out over the pond alongside the living room. The open passageway at the far end of the room leads to the family room (§48).

§67 The rectangular pond alongside the living room divides the front part of the garden from a more private and informal section in the rear, outside the family room (§68). ▷

§68 The small family room behind the dining room has wall-to-wall glass doors opening on the private garden, which is paved with wooden bricks.

§69 A view from the balcony outside the second-floor bedrooms shows the garden, its pond, and the wooden terrace beside the living room. The balcony terminates in a sun deck, partly visible at the upper right.

§70 The master bedroom has painted muslin walls and a cloth ceiling. Large glass doors open on the balcony that runs the length of the south side of the second floor.

HOUSE OF BRICK AND CHESTNUT

Architects: Design Section, Takenaka Construction Co.
Location: Minato-ku, Tokyo
Builders: Takenaka Construction Co.
Site area: 21,916 square feet
Building area: 4,689 square feet
Total floor area: 6,600 square feet
Estimated cost: Not obtainable

AS NOTED in the first volume of *Contemporary Japanese Houses*, it is an unfortunate fact that few of the large, expensive houses built in Japan in the postwar period have been distinguished in the architectural sense. Here is an exception: a small mansion with a half-acre garden, designed with care, skill, excellent taste, and no nonsense.

The title is perhaps misleading, for the house is, as the pictures show, not made of brick and chestnut wood, but of ferroconcrete, finished on most of the outside with mortar. Still, the character of the building and, to some extent, its unity derive largely from an ample use of rough-finished brick and natural chestnut. The ceilings, including those under the projecting eaves, are all of the latter material, and brick walls and wainscoting are to be found here and there both inside and out. One of the most striking features of the living-dining area is a large brick installation that appears at a glance to be a fireplace and hearth, but is in fact an air return for the heating-and-cooling system (§74).

The house has a large covered carport and entranceway (with chestnut ceilings, of course) culminating in an impressive entrance hall (§73). A door on the left side of this hall leads to a ground-level parlor where callers who need not be invited into the living room are received. This room has a large picture window looking out on an artificial pond and, beyond that, a gravel-and-rock garden with one immense tree (§71).

A short stairway leads from the entrance hall up to the main living section, where there is a big living room on the south (§74 & COLOR §11) and a dining room on the north (§75). The two rooms are actually one space, divided only by the brick air return mentioned above and a slight difference in floor and ceiling levels. Broad glass doors at the east end of the living room lead to a covered terrace, which in turn leads to the garden. A rectangular section of the garden directly south of the living room and terrace has been built up to nearly the same level as the floor inside, but the remainder of the garden is several feet lower than the house. There are, in effect, three gardens: the rock-and-gravel garden by the entrance and receiving room, the raised garden outside the living room, and a more private garden in the innermost part of the lot. In addition, there is a small semi-enclosed garden on the north side of the house, beside the dining room (§75).

Bedrooms for the owner and his wife are at the west end of the first floor, and there are three bedrooms for the children on the second floor. A balcony runs from the living-room terrace down the south and west sides of the first-floor bedrooms, and two of the upstairs rooms open on a sun deck above the living room.

Noteworthy features of the design are the changes in floor level as one goes from one area to another and the use in several places of skylights through which light is thrown at night from electric lamps on the roof (§76).

◁ *§71 A view from the southeast shows the receiving room at ground level, bordered on three sides by a pond, and the living room at a somewhat higher level. The garden outside the living room is built up nearly to the interior floor level.*

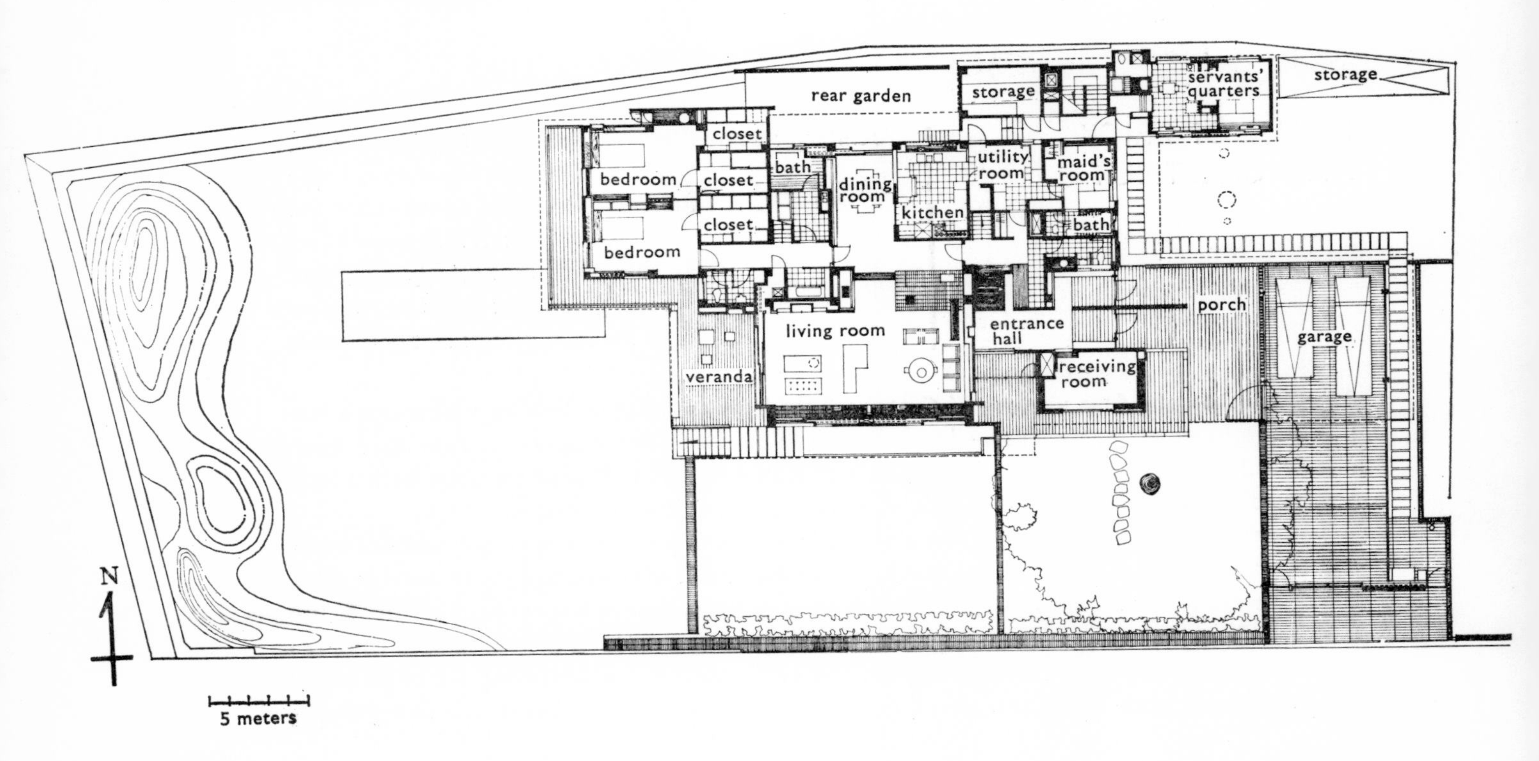

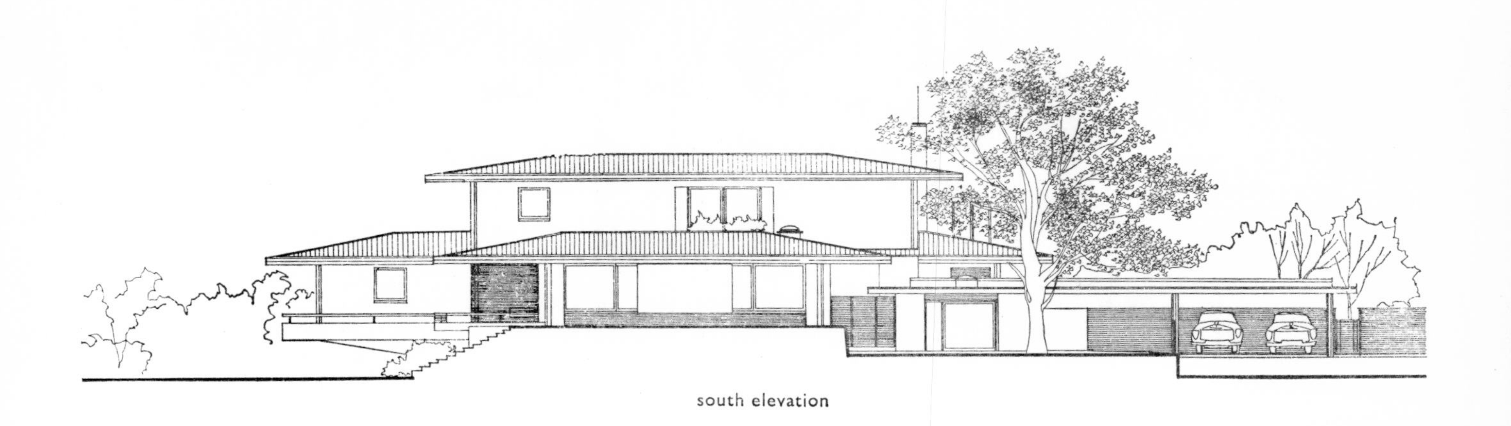

south elevation

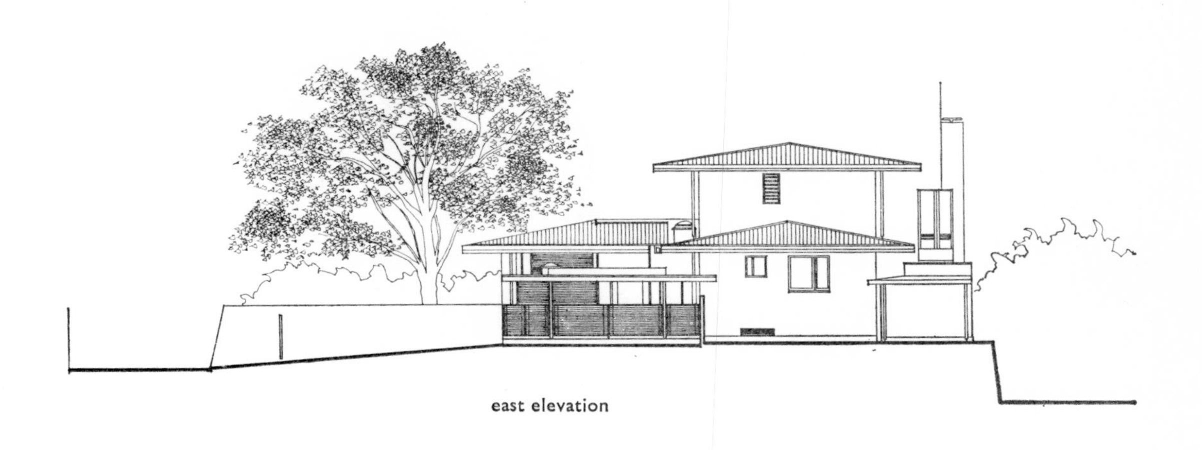

east elevation

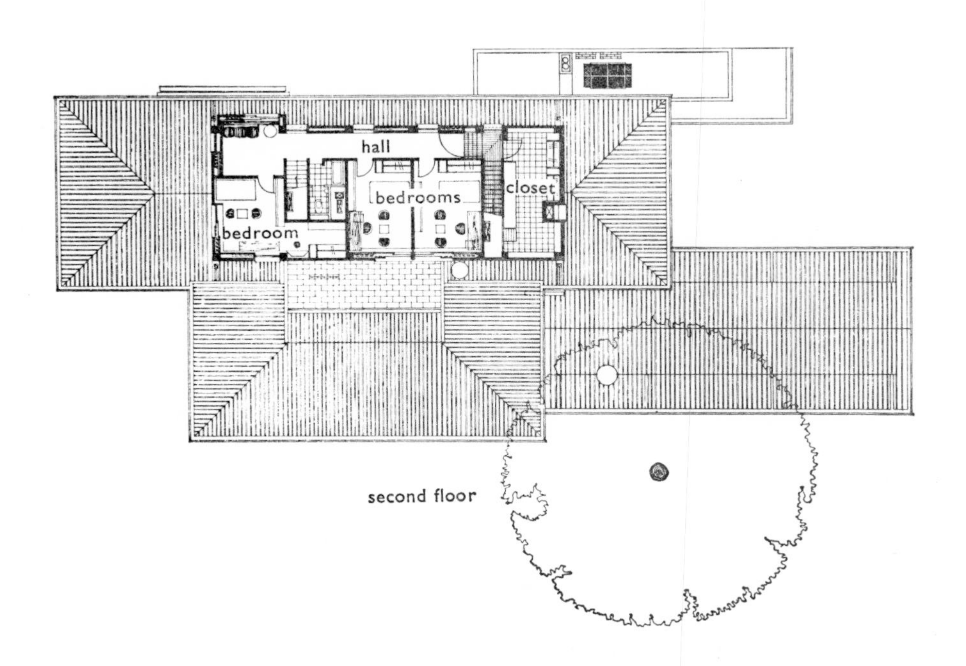

second floor

§72 At the west end of the house are a wing for bedrooms and a spacious covered terrace. The roofing is of copper, and the ceilings are of chestnut, as in the interior. The room at the right is the living room (see COLOR *§11). A stairway, hidden by the bush in the foreground, leads down a few steps to the rear garden.*

§73 At the far end of the large entrance hall is a brick wall with ▷ a lighted niche for an art object. The large window at the left overlooks the pond seen in §71, and a stairway at the right leads up to the main living quarters. The doorway in the left foreground is the entrance to the receiving room.

§74 The living room (foreground) and the dining room are essentially a single space, though they have different floor and ceiling levels. The hearth-like brick construction at the center of the photograph is the air return for the air-conditioning system. Light from the round skylight above streams down into the "fireplace," which is open at the top.

COLOR §11 *The large living room is more or less divided in two by the low table left of center, the area in the foreground being somewhat more formal than that adjacent to the terrace. The walls visible here are covered with cloth, but this alternates with chestnut paneling and rough-finished brick in other parts of the room. The brick wainscot on the south side runs the length of the room.*

§75 A brick wall on one side of the dining room echos the wall beyond the small garden north of the room. The door on the right leads to the kitchen, to the west of which are the fairly extensive servants' quarters.

§76 A night view from the south shows two upstairs bedrooms, the living room (left), the stairway from the entrance hall to the living room, and the receiving room. Electric lamps at the right throw light through circular skylights into the interior.

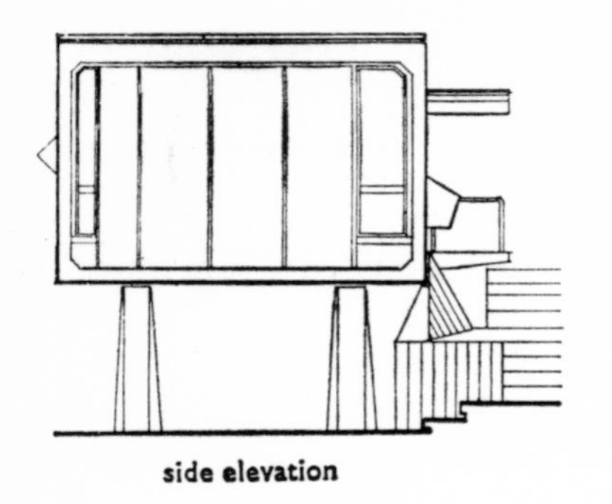

side elevation

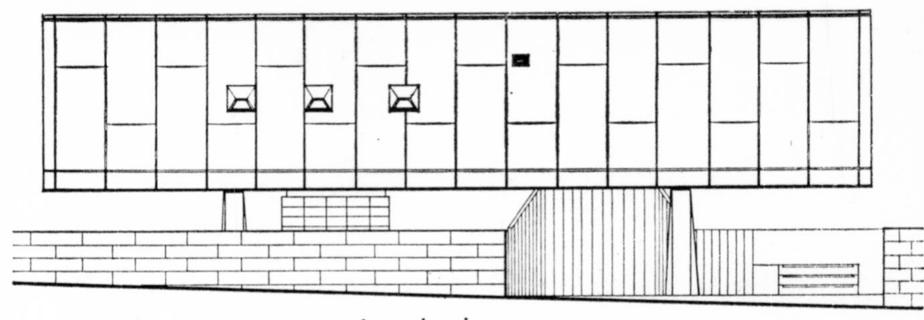

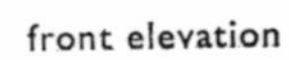

front elevation

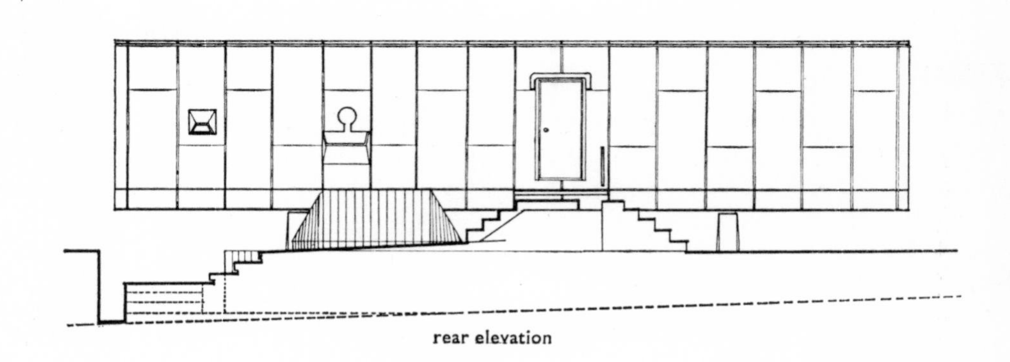

rear elevation

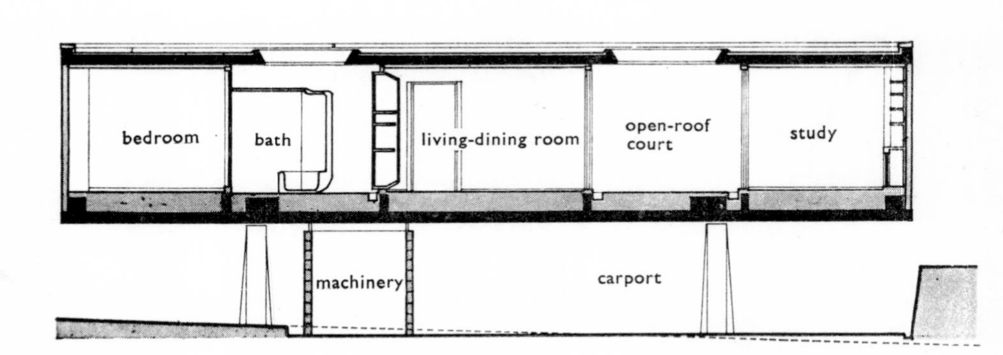

CONCRETE BOX FOR THE CITY

Architects: RIA Group
Location: Nakameguro, Tokyo
Builders: Iwamoto Construction Co.
Site area: 1,076 square feet
Building area: 802 square feet
Floor area: 6 square feet
Estimated cost: $720.00

IN ALL LARGE Japanese cities, and particularly in Tokyo and Osaka, one of the problems most frequently encountered by designers of houses is that of providing privacy on small lots facing busy streets. Here the solution was simply to encase the whole house in a concrete box, whose walls are broken only by small openings intended to provide ventilation or means of emergency exit.

The lot has an area of only about 1,000 square feet and a depth of only about twenty feet from the edge of the street in front. The parents of the owner live in an older house farther in from the street and at a slightly higher ground level. Largely to ensure good communication between the two houses, the designers set the new building on *pilotis* high enough to allow for entrance, parking space, and a machinery room underneath (§§77 & 79).

Inside the box there are three basic living spaces, alternating with two open-roof courts, which furnish the principal source of natural light for the interior, as well as its only view of the exterior—or of the sky, to be exact. The central room serves as kitchen, dining room, and living room (§80). Since the occupants, a couple with no children, are away most of the day, this space is on the whole utilitarian and tends to be dominated by the need for eating, though it is given a certain graciousness by full-length, full-width glass doors on one side, opening onto one of the light courts (§81). Beyond this court is a relatively spacious study (§82), where the owner, a scholar, can work in the evenings and on weekends. At the other end of the house is the bedroom, linked to the living room by a narrow utility room. The court between the living room and the bedroom is largely occupied by a manufactured unit containing bath, lavatory, and toilet (§83).

This "machine for living" is another example of the strong influence enjoyed in Japan by the coiner of that phrase, Le Corbusier. *Pilotis*, exposed concrete exterior, roof gardens, and what someone has described as "little Corbusier windows" are all present. Rather than describe the style as "derivative," however, it would be fairer to say that many of the more prominent features of Le Corbusier's buildings have by now become part and parcel of the vocabulary of contemporary Japanese architecture—just as traditional wooden post-and-beam structures are a part of that vocabulary—and are used freely as the occasion demands.

The noises and intrusions of modern Japanese cities are such that extreme means of separating the interior from the exterior are fast gaining in favor, and this house has a simple and straightforward integrity that will command attention from all urban architects challenged by problems similar to the ones it presented. It also has a personality, which, though somewhat formidable, is yet an admirable expression of the proposition that man's home is his own, and not a public thoroughfare.

◁ *§77 The house presents an almost blank wall of concrete to the street, with only small openings for ventilation. The primary sources of natural light for the interior are two "light gardens" that are open to the sky. The heaviness of the long concrete mass is mitigated by the* pilotis *arrangement, which also provides space underneath for parking, the main entranceway, and a small machinery room.*

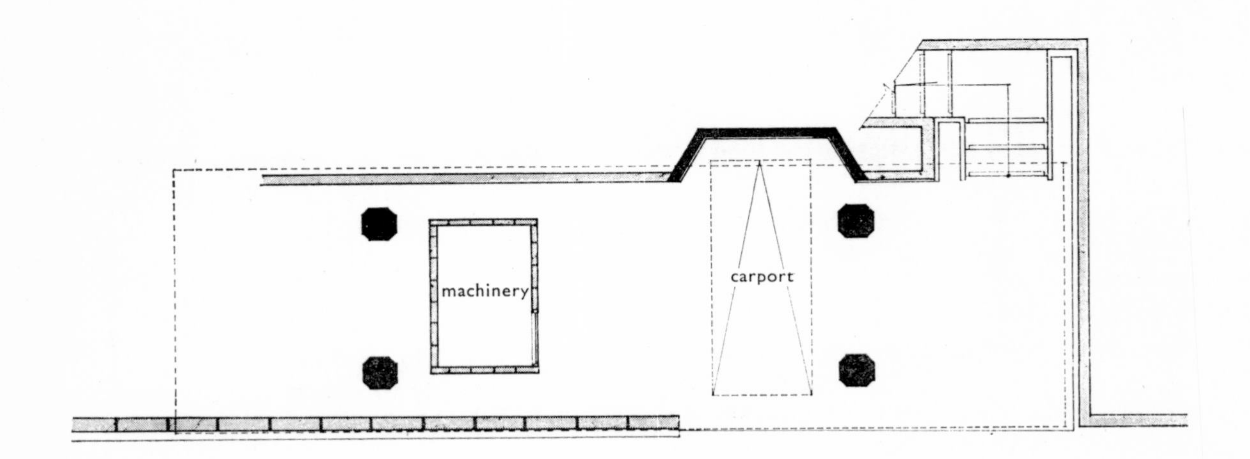

§78 Four massive pilotis *raise the building to a height of about seven feet above the street, exposing a floor slab whose under surface is like that of the exterior walls.*

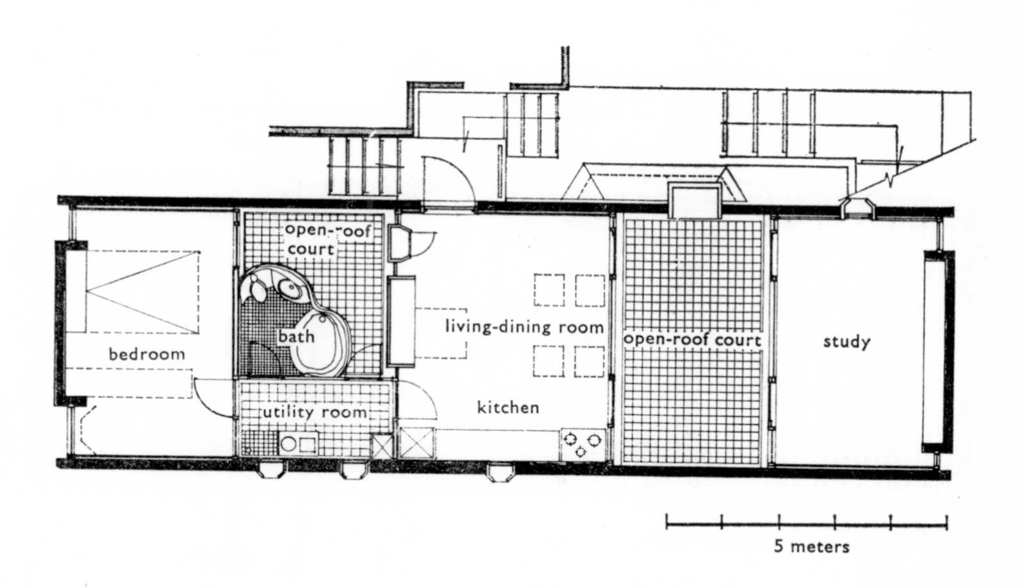

§80 The central room is primarily kitchen and dining room, but it has a cabinet for a television and a hi-fi set. The light at the upper center comes from the court between this room and the bedroom. The latter is visible in the distance through the doorways at the left.

§81 Both the central living room and the owner's study have full-length, full-width openings on one of the two light courts. The court will eventually be "landscaped" with plants to form an eminently urban garden.

◁ *§79 A close-up of the back side of the house shows a fanciful sculptured opening in the wall of the court between the living-dining room and the study. The gate at the lower left opens on the street. Concrete walls have acquired a rough texture from the wooden shuttering in which they were poured.*

§82 An opaque-glass window in the master's study offers means of emergency escape, as well as additional light, without breaking the closed-exterior concept that underlies the design.

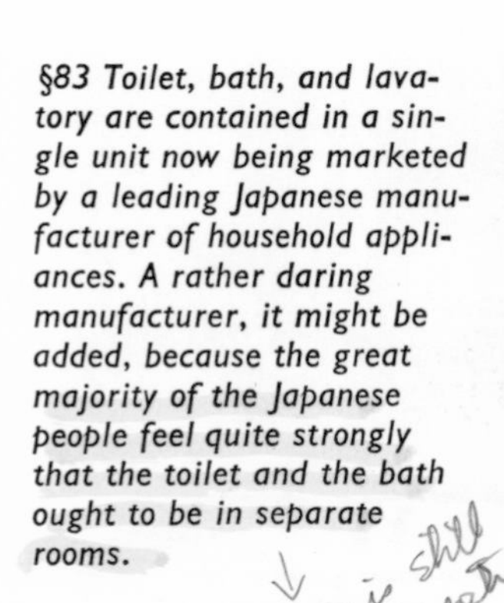

§83 Toilet, bath, and lavatory are contained in a single unit now being marketed by a leading Japanese manufacturer of household appliances. A rather daring manufacturer, it might be added, because the great majority of the Japanese people feel quite strongly that the toilet and the bath ought to be in separate rooms.

HOUSE WITH LAMINATED BEAMS

Architects: RIA Group
Location: Ashiya, Hyōgo Prefecture
Builders: Sakai Construction Co.
Site area: 7,130 square feet
Building area: 2,924 square feet
Floor area: 2,094 square feet
Estimated cost: $33,330.00

THE LOCATION is in Ashiya, one of the better suburbs of Osaka, where the Rokkō Mountains form a background on the north, and the land slopes gently down to the sea on the south. Though the site has a good view in this direction, it presented problems, since it was not only small for the house required, but was also divided down the north-south axis by a small stream.

The designers decided to cover nearly the whole lot with the roof and to allow the house to straddle the stream. To secure a large span, they made use of laminated beams that curve upward toward the middle of the building proper to accommodate a rise in floor level from the east to the west side (§84). The long east-west span made possible a spacious and open section on the south containing a living room (§87), a combination dining and family room (§§89 & 90), and a large covered terrace, walled in on the street side (§86).

Behind this public section, the kitchen, maid's room, baths, and private bedrooms are grouped in an L-shaped plan. Sufficient space was left on the north for parking and for a walk approaching the entrance (§85). On the south, a veranda runs the length of the house.

This house is unusual in that its only tatami-floored room belongs to the maid. As a result, the building could, to all intents and purposes, be a bungalow in the coastal hills of California, rather than a Japanese dwelling. Certain features, however, conciliate the Japanese tradition, among them the southern orientation, the entrance hall where shoes are removed, the veranda along the open side, the large sliding doors, and the inner court (§88) that adds so much charm and visual comfort to the living room.

◁ *§84 The entire east (right) side of the house is higher than the west side, and a small stream flows underneath the building at the point where the change in level takes place. Curving laminated beams reduce the abruptness of the rise and permit a smoothly flowing roof line. The roof and ceiling are again lowered somewhat over the bedroom at the far right, which forms the foot of an L-shaped sector containing the more private rooms of the house. At the left the roof extends beyond the house to cover the terrace.*

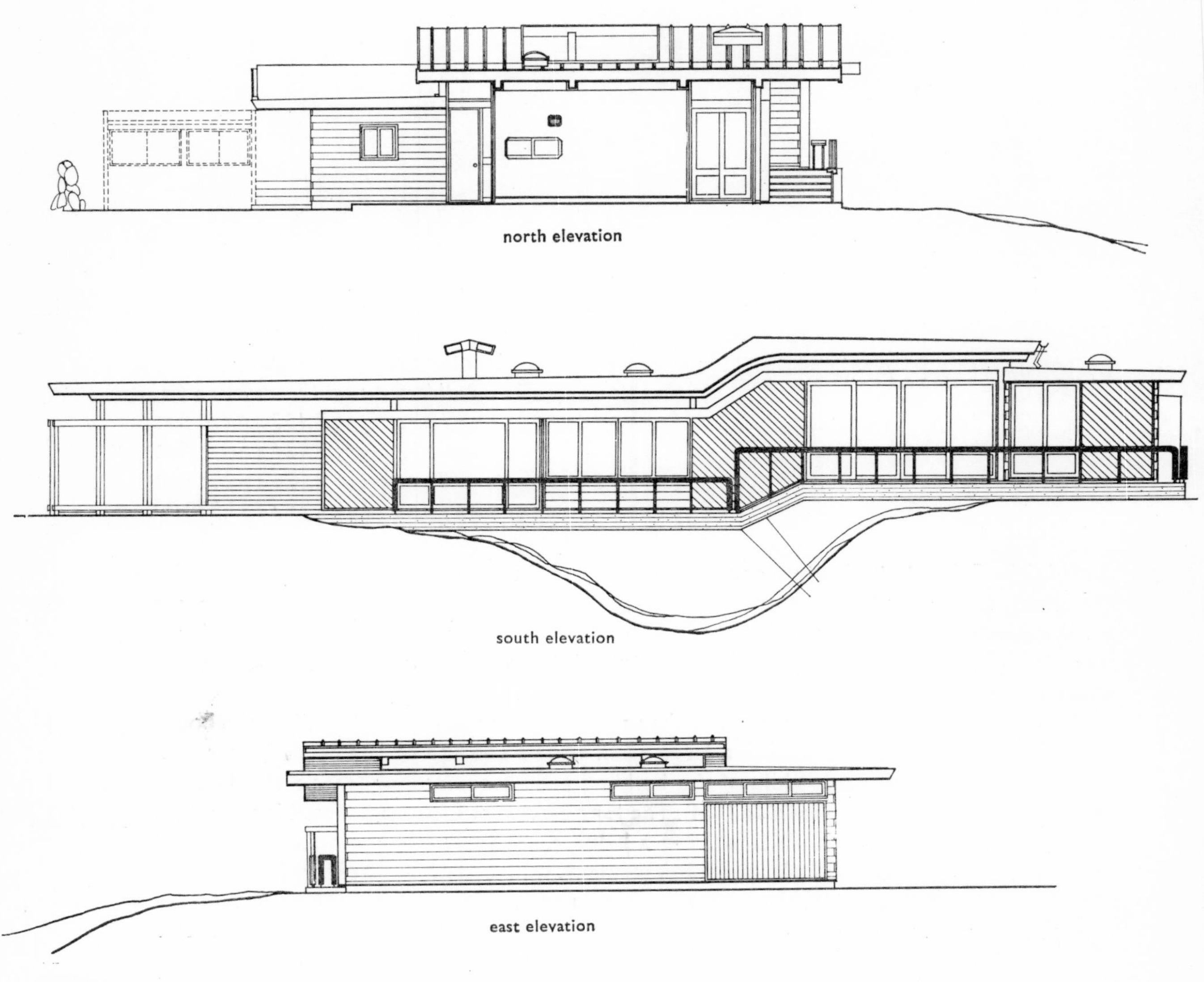

§85 *On the north side of the lot, which is at the same level as the road, space was left for an entranceway and a carport. Otherwise, the site is almost completely covered by the large-span roof.*

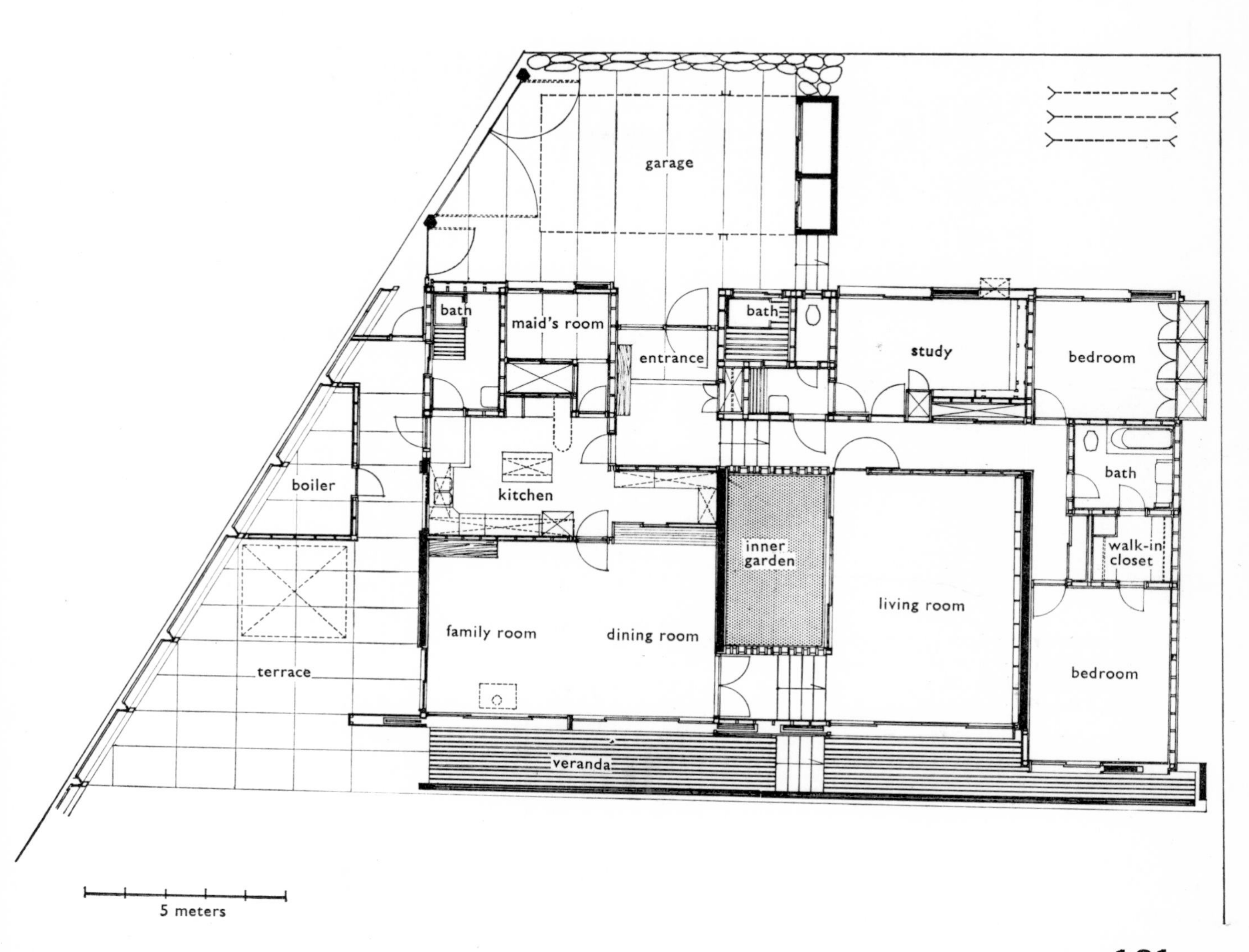

§86 The property was built up somewhat on the west, and a retaining wall was made of local stone. Above this, a wooden wall isolates the terrace outside the family room from the adjacent road. The square opening in the roof provides overhead light for the terrace.

§87 The living room has a picture window on the south, where the view is best. The wall at the left, which separates the living room from the master bedroom is of plaster covered with Oya stone, a soft Japanese rock of grayish hue. The light in the foreground is from the open-roof inner court.

§88 The plastic curve of the beam across the skylight enhances the sculptural effect of the inner court, which provides light for both the living room and, through a grilled window on the far left, a hallway on the north.

§89 At the lower end of the house, several steps down from the living room, is a combination dining and informal sitting room with a fireplace. As in the living room, there are large openings on the south (right).

§90 The family room opens onto the spacious stone-paved terrace, which is continuous with the narrow wooden veranda on the south side of the house.

SUBURBAN HOUSE

Architect: Tetsuya Hayashi
Location: Kamakura, Kanagawa Prefecture
Builders: Sakazumi Construction Co.
Site area: 6,413 square feet
Building area: 1,796 square feet
*Estimated cost: **$16,310.00***

MANY OF THE world's great cities, particularly in the United States, have been troubled by the exodus of the population to suburbia. In Japan there has also been a movement toward the suburbs, but by no means a deliberate one. Basically, most Japanese who work in the larger urban districts would prefer to live as close to the center of things as possible, but the scarcity and high cost of centrally located property has made inevitable a vast sprawl into the suburban areas.

In the past twenty years about twenty percent of the Japanese population has moved from the country to the city, and the six or seven largest urban centers, which were already troubled with housing shortages before this implosion began, have so far found no better practical solution than simply to spread and spread and spread. Areas once considered appropriate for country houses are now in many instances the next thing to "downtown."

Suburban housing has assumed two basic forms: the *danchi* and the *bunjō-chi*. The *danchi* is a large complex of rented apartment houses, usually having its own stores and other public facilities. The *bunjō-chi*, on the other hand, is what is commonly known in the United States as a "housing development project," which is to say an area in which a large entrepreneur or landholder (occasionally the government) undertakes to create a new neighborhood by selling off land in small parcels to prospective house-owners. Sometimes the owner offers a package deal, in which a house is included with the land. More often, however, he does no more than make the area habitable by providing streets and electricity and leaves it to the purchaser of the land to build his own residence.

The house shown here is in such a *bunjō-chi*, located about an hour by train from Tokyo. The site, which is on a hillside, affords a good view to the south and is on the whole pleasant, although the new owner-builders in the vicinity have only begun to landscape their lots, and the new-turned earth is still rather stark.

The designer provided a simple, straightforward plan in which the more public rooms are on the south and the private ones on the north. The long, low roof line and extensive openings on the front (§§92 & 96; COLOR §12) are in no way extraordinary in postwar residential architecture, but the curve of the roof as seen from the side (§91) is a departure from the usual rectilinear pattern, and one that seems to emphasize the role of the house as a protective shelter.

By way of contrast to the hovering roof, the rooms themselves are very open (§95). The focal point that pulls the whole plan together is a semi-covered porch in the middle of the south side (§97). A pool between this porch and the dining room adds an element of surprise and playfulness.

◁ *§91 The view from the street on the west reveals a gently curved roof line, which is an innovation in Japanese house design. The opening in the roof at left center and the flower box beneath it separate the garage from the entranceway.*

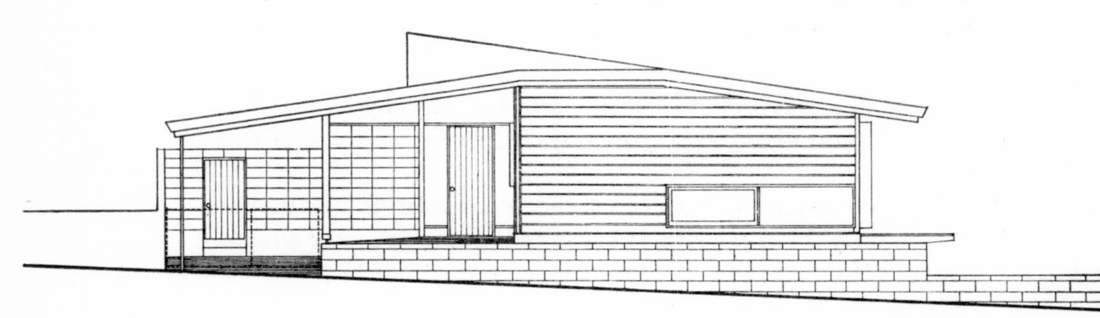

west elevation

§92 The house has broad openings on the south, where a garden is taking form. The straight, low-slung roof line and the large glass panels relate this building to the style described in the first volume of Contemporary Japanese Houses *as "neo-Japanese"—a post-war innovation noted for its lightness and economy of expression.*

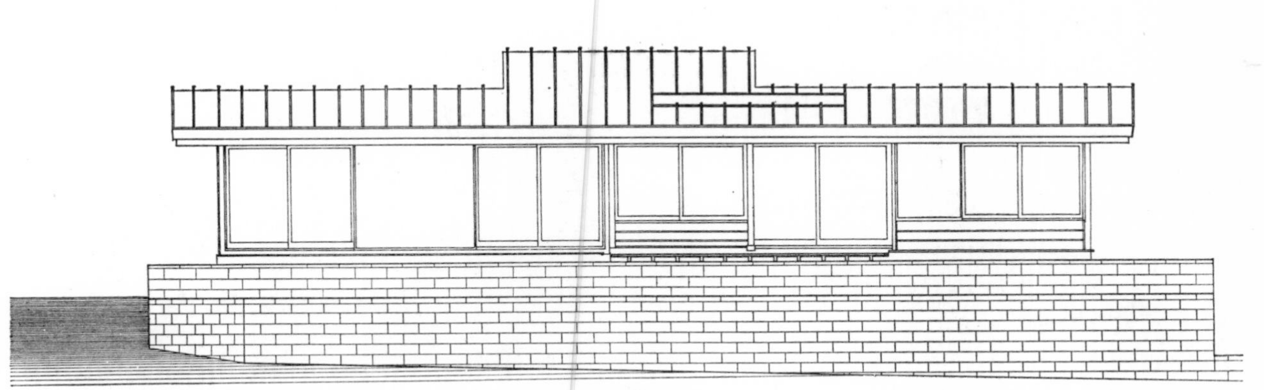

south elevation

§94 The tiled entrance hall has glass walls that gradualize the ▷ passage from outside to inside.

§93 Stone steps lead from the carport to the main entrance at the upper left. The chain at the left is a guide for rainwater falling from the opening in the roof above the flower box. The stepping stones at the right lead around the house to the garden on the south.

§95 The natural color of the wooden walls and ceilings is emphasized in the living room. Both the living room and the Japanese-style room to the right have large doors opening on the garden.

COLOR §12 *The doors in the large opening on the south side of the living room can be slid back entirely out of view, as can the shoji between the living room and the porch. When all the doors are open, the living room, porch, and stone terrace form an integrated, but varied, three-level space that is a happy medium between interior and exterior.*

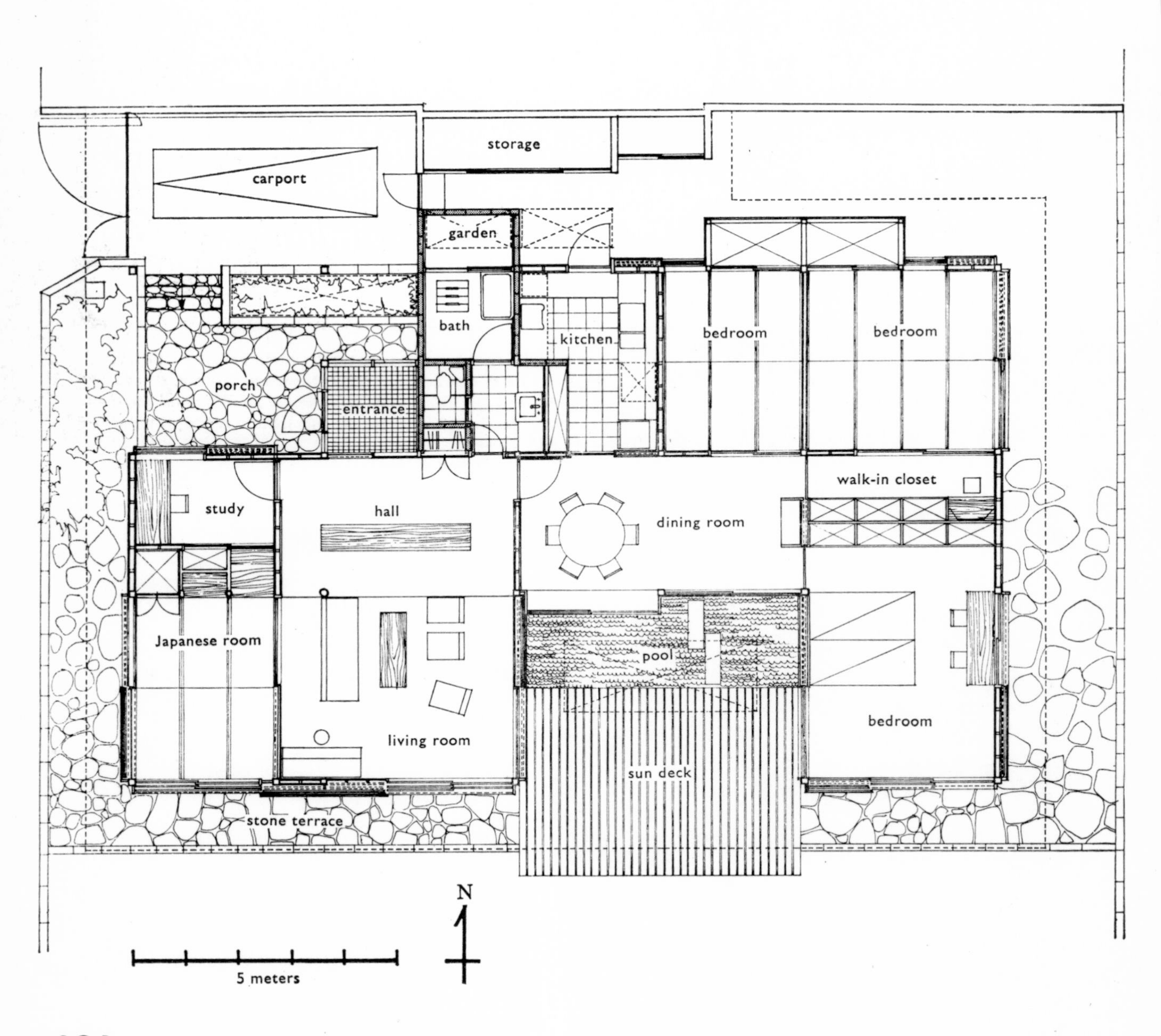
storage
carport
garden
bath
kitchen
bedroom
bedroom
porch
entrance
walk-in closet
study
hall
dining room
Japanese room
pool
bedroom
living room
sun deck
stone terrace
N
5 meters

§96 The centrally located porch, which can be approached directly from the living room (left, behind the shoji), the dining room (center), and the front bedroom (right), is a focal point of the design. Between the porch and the dining room is a small pool, lighted by a rectangular opening in the roof.

§97 The dark area in the foreground is the shallow pool between the dining room and the porch. At night the pool can be lighted with small spotlights.

WEEKEND HOUSE

Architect: Junzō Yoshimura
Location: Itō, Shizuoka Prefecture
Builders: Seto Construction Co.
Site area: 15,571 square feet
Building area: 2,015 square feet
Total floor area: 2,301 square feet
Estimated cost: $16,670.00

THOUGH THIS house is described as a weekend house, the owner plans eventually to make it his year-round residence, and the design is consequently less casual than is normal for Japanese country houses. This may, in effect, be regarded as a suburban dwelling that happens to have a particularly beautiful setting.

The site is at the top of a small mountain near the eastern shore of the Izu Peninsula, and the view is spectacular. To the east and south is the Pacific Ocean with an array of islands, to the west, the lofty Amagi Range of Central Izu, and to the north, Mount Omuro. To take advantage of this panorama, the designer provided ample fenestration on all sides, and particularly on the south, where the view is best (§§98 & 100).

The house is essentially a one-story frame building, but it rests on a concrete foundation that follows the rise and fall of the terrain, and at both east and west ends, where the ground is lower than in the middle, it was possible to provide concrete-enclosed cellars, one serving as a laundry and machine room, and the other as a storage room. There was also space underneath the east wing of the house for a carport (§99).

The nucleus of the plan is a large living-dining room (§102 & COLOR §13) with sliding windows all across the south side and smaller fixed windows on the other three sides. Adjacent to the dining room area is the kitchen, which has no outside openings, but is amply lighted and ventilated by a large skylight. At the east and west ends of the house are suites of Japanese rooms (§§103 & 104), and on the north side is a spacious toilet-and-bath area. The bath is supplied with water from an adjacent hot spring.

Junzō Yoshimura is known in the United States as the designer of the Motel on the Mountain, just north of New York City. Those who have seen the restaurant at the Motel will recognize in this weekend house many of the same quietly expert features seen there, in particular the broad openings that draw the landscape into the building, the easy use of natural textures, and the excellent proportions.

◁ *§98 The site is at the top of a hill, and a concrete platform was built to create a level foundation for the one-story frame building. At the east and west ends, where the ground is lower, it was possible to provide concrete-enclosed cellars and a carport.*

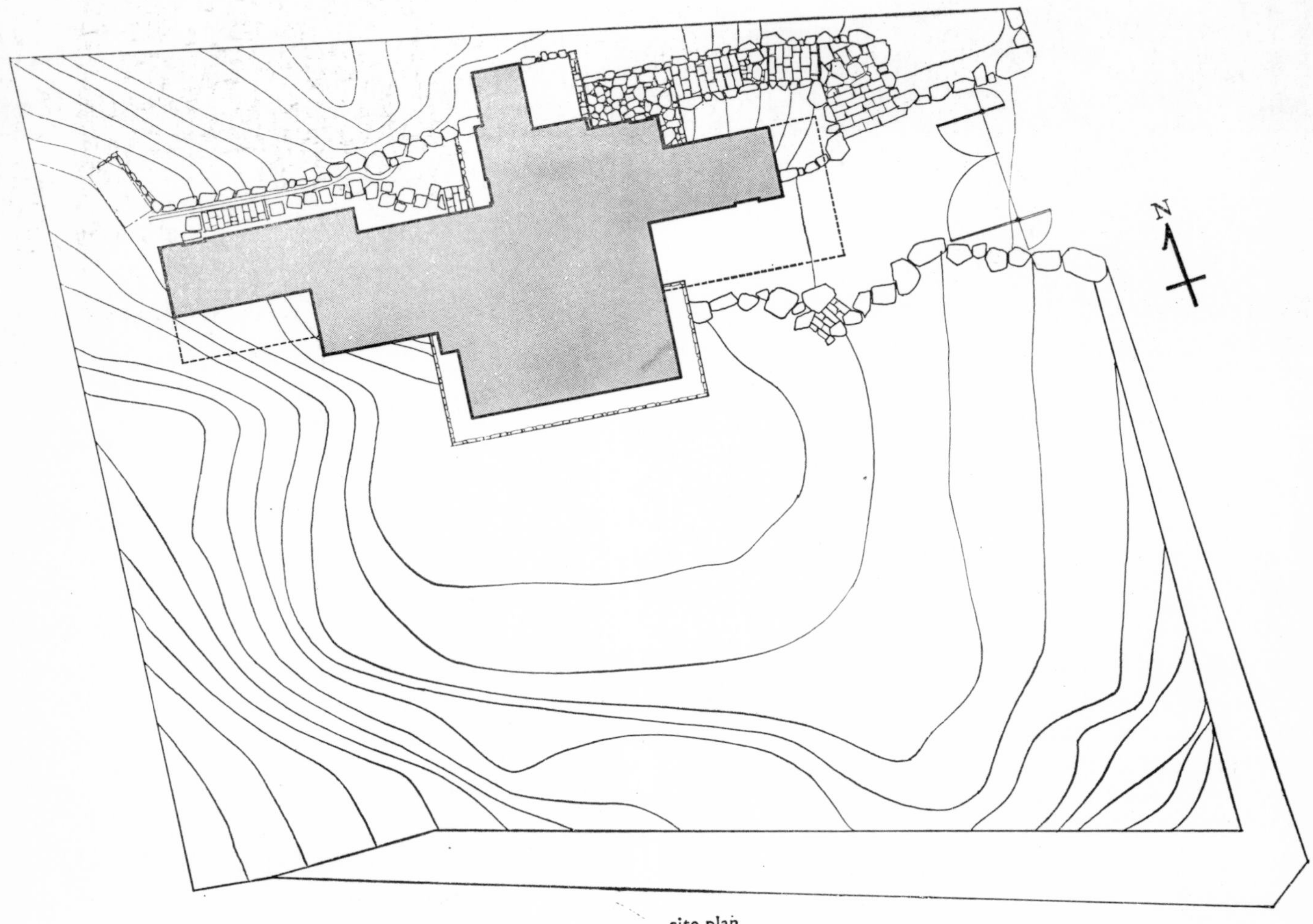

site plan

§99 The stone steps at the right lead up to the entrance on the north side, and the door beside the automobile opens into the laundry. The east bedroom suite is above.

§100 Stone steps on the west side of the living room lead down to the front garden, which is in the process of being landscaped.

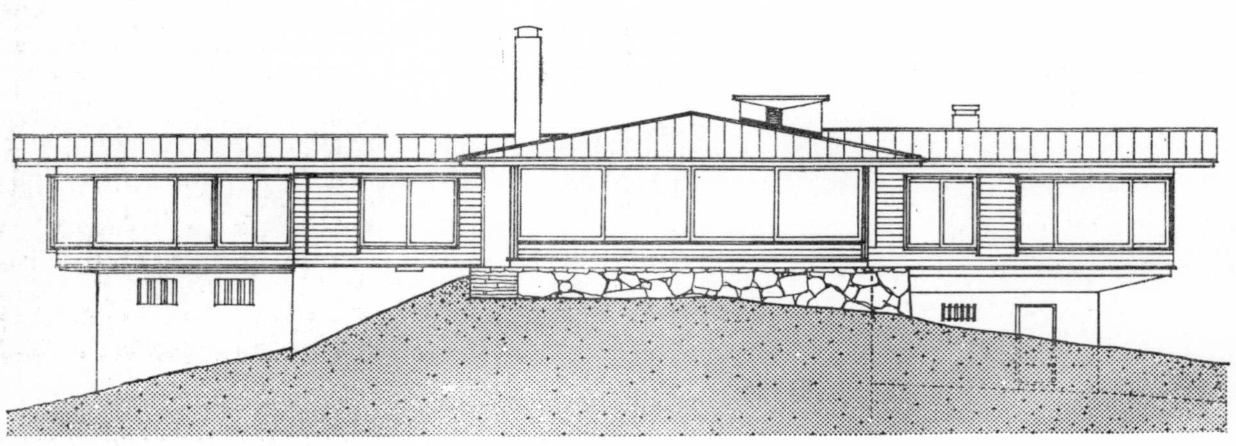

south elevation

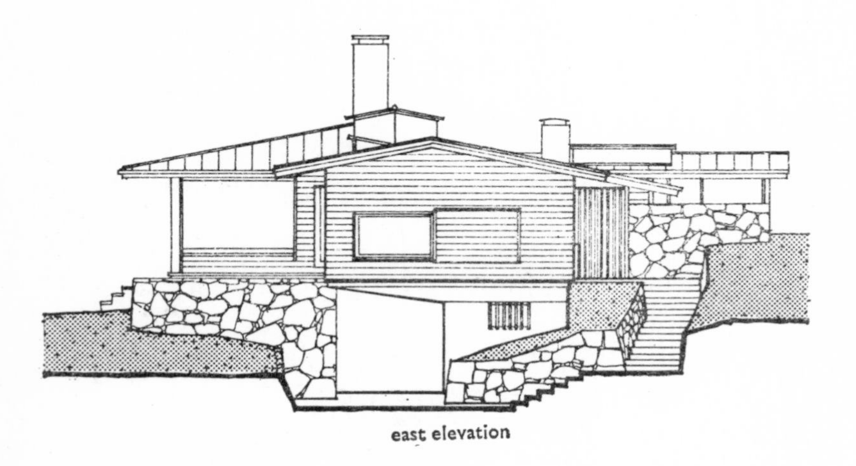

east elevation

§101 The ledge outside the living room is known in Japanese as inu-bashiri, or "place for the dog to run." In this house it is a convenient place to stand when closing the rain shutters or washing the windows. ▷

§102 The large living room has sliding windows all across the south side and fixed panes on the other three sides. To reduce visual obstructions, the frames of the sliding windows have been concealed behind the structure and wainscoting.

COLOR §13 *Indirect lighting is concealed behind the boards above the windows. The slanting part of the ceiling is of cryptomeria wood, and the upper part is covered with cloth. Traditional Japanese clay is used for all the walls except the one framing the fireplace, which is of a soft rock called Oya stone.*

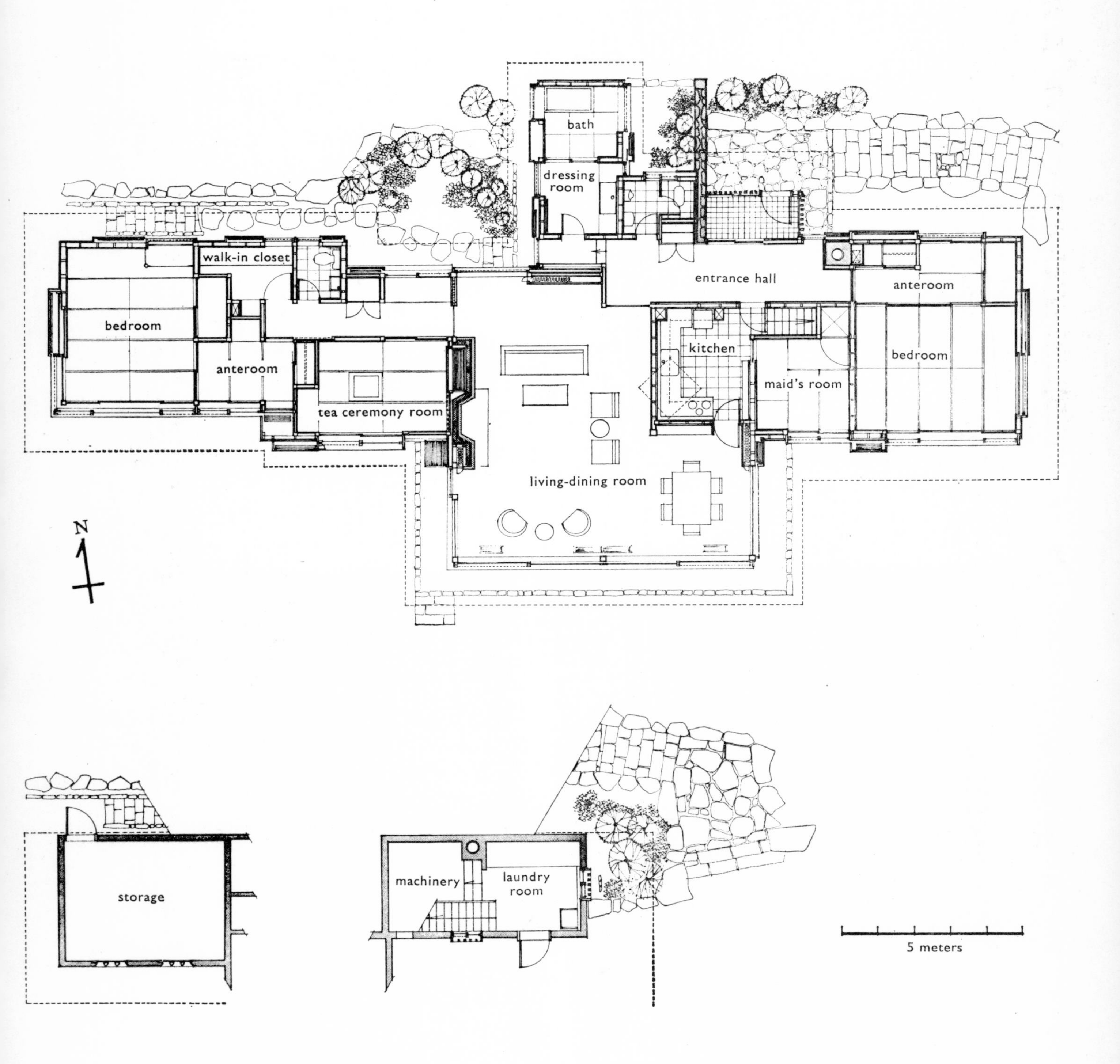
bath
dressing room
walk-in closet
entrance hall
anteroom
bedroom
kitchen
bedroom
anteroom
maid's room
tea ceremony room
living-dining room
N
storage
machinery
laundry room
5 meters

§103 The main bedroom, which is at the west end of the house, has corner windows facing south and west.

§104 Next to the living room is a six-mat tearoom with a hearth in the floor and a traditional pothook suspended from the ceiling.

HOUSE WITH FIR TREES

Architect: Antonin Raymond
Location: Karuizawa, Nagano Prefecture
Builders: Karuizawa Construction Co.
Site area: 32,400 square feet
Building area: 2,582 square feet
Estimated cost: $27,780.00

FEW SPOTS in the well-known summer resort of Karuizawa are as beautiful as the sloping site of this house, which is endowed not only with an impressive stand of trees, but with a view toward the southeast of a lovely mountain stream and waterfall. Into this setting the designer, Antonin Raymond, working with the able assistance of his wife Noemi, has nestled an informal, but well-organized building that blends with the terrain and the view (§105), while at the same time harmonizing easily in texture with the quiet wooded surroundings and the large fir trees that have given the house its name.

About a third of the total floor area is occupied by a living room and dining room (§§109 & 110; COLOR §14), which are separated only by large sliding panels and can be combined to form a single space when necessary. The dining room is further linked spatially with the kitchen by a service window opening on a counter in the hallway (§111). Dining room, living room, and master bedroom all open onto a wide railless veranda (§§106 & 107) that serves as a pleasant transition from interior to exterior.

The entrance hall, a section for the kitchen and the maid's room, and a Japanese-style bath are contained in three separate extensions on the north side of the house, and the bath has its own private little garden, surrounded with a bamboo fence (§112). At the west end of the house is a guest room, and at the east end, a pair of bedrooms for the younger people in the family. This latter section is at a lower ground level than the rest of the building.

As in his earlier Country House with Thatched Roof (*Contemporary Japanese Houses*, Vol. I, pp. 139–152), Raymond has built the principal framework of the house of logs and left the underside of the roof exposed in the main rooms. Typically, he has employed split-log braces for the roof structure, so that the upper space in the living room and dining room becomes a sort of wooden-frame vault, adding greatly to the appeal of the interior. In the large fireplace and hearth he has combined unfinished concrete with stone from the surrounding vicinity. Local stone is also used for paving in the entranceway (§108) and in a covered terrace that is shared by the living room and the guest room. Aesthetic emphasis throughout the house is on the natural appearance and textures of the building materials.

Raymond is possibly the most skillful architect in the world at applying the principles of traditional Japanese wooden architecture to houses that are in a functional sense essentially Western, and this building is but one more example of his ability in this respect.

◁ *§105 On the south side of the house the land slopes down toward a stream with a waterfall. The living room (left of the bench on the veranda) was placed so as to have the best possible view, and other rooms were arranged on either side of it in a line that curves gently around the garden.*

§106 At the west end of the house (foreground) both the guest bedroom (far left) and the living room open on a covered terrace paved with local stone. ▷

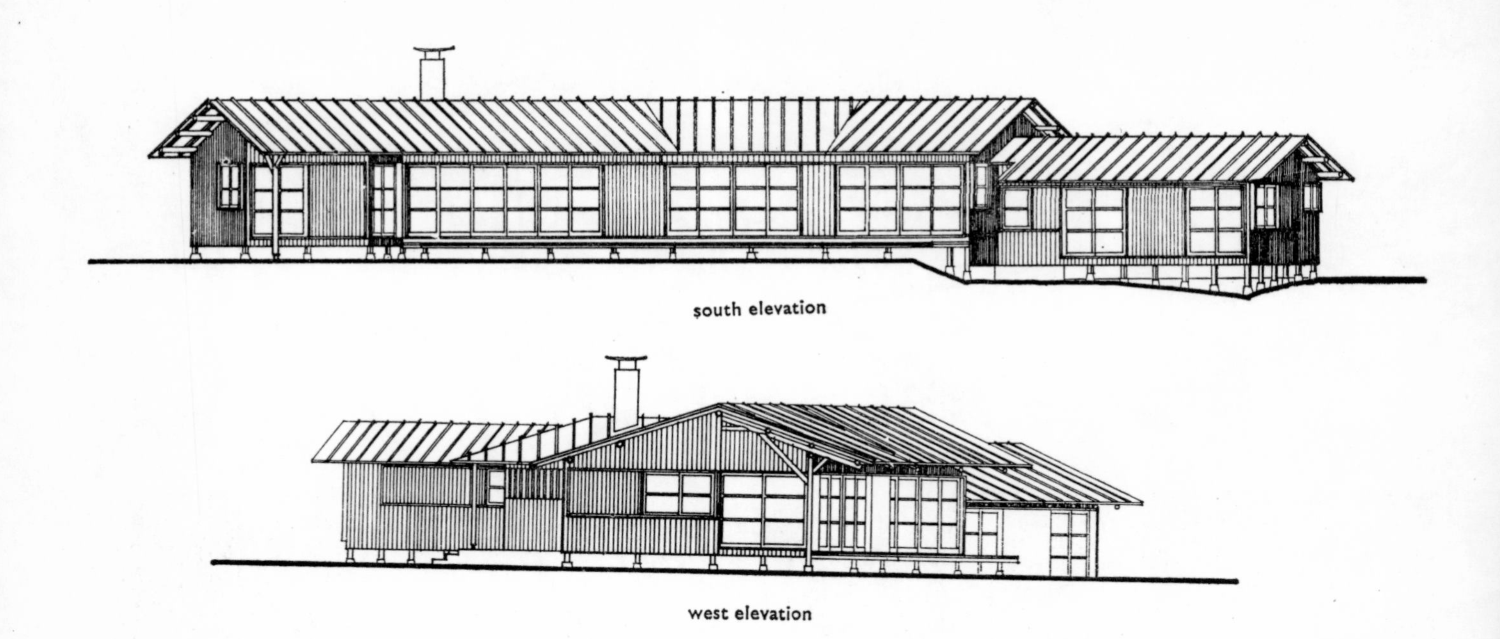

south elevation

west elevation

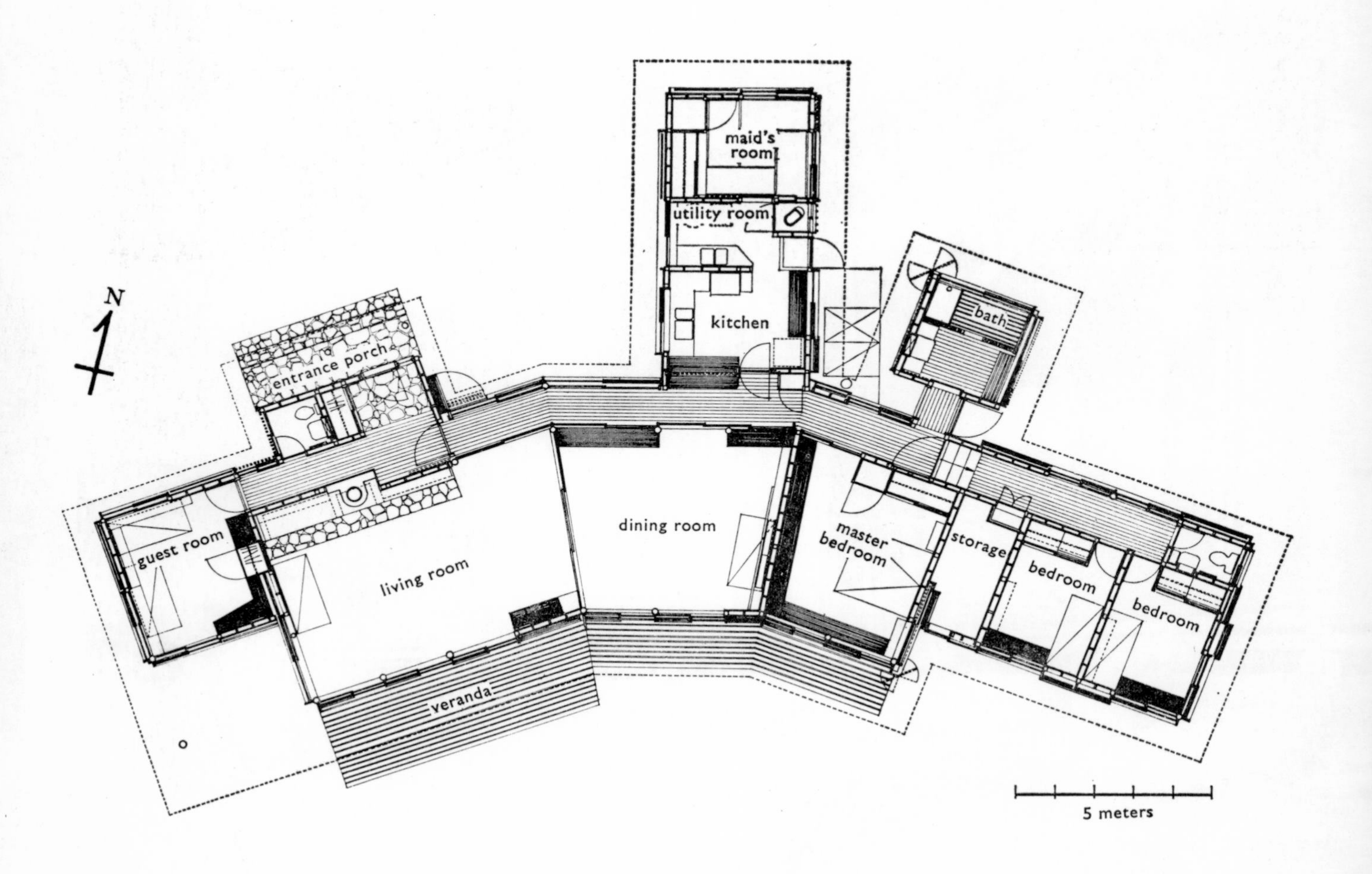

§107 The veranda (sunoko-en) on the south provides an excellent place for outdoor relaxation, and at the same time serves as an exterior line between the three rooms in the central sector of the house. The floor of the veranda is of elm, the structure of larch, and the exterior walls of American pine.

COLOR §14 *The living room can be combined with the dining room by removing the sliding panels at the right. The walls are of lauan, while the structure is of larch, and the floor of elm. The split-log diagonal braces along the sides of the room are a typical Raymond touch.*

◁ §108 *The entrance porch, which is paved with local stone, is covered by the long extension of the eaves. The front door is at the far right. Straight ahead is the wing containing the kitchen and the maid's room.*

§109 A view of the living room from the dining room shows the large fireplace and chimney sculpted from unfinished concrete and local stone. The main heating is not supplied by the fireplace, but from a central system with ducts under the floor. The sliding panels at the right are covered with handmade Japanese paper.

§110 The connecting hallway on the north is virtually an integral part of the living-dining area, being separated from it only by low built-in cabinets and shoji. The shoji on the outer side of the hall open on a garden between the kitchen wing and the entrance porch.

§111 A counter in the hallway next to the east end of the dining room can be connected with the kitchen by raising a pair of paper-covered panels.

§112 A Japanese-style bath, with a deep wooden tub (left), opens on a small garden fenced in with bamboo. The bath water is heated by a boiler outside the house to the left of the tub. The mallet-like device on top of the tub is for stirring the water as it is heated.

ON STILTS IN THE MOUNTAINS

Architects: Akio Yamamoto and Tsutomu Ikuta
Location: Tadeshina Heights, Nagano Prefecture
Builder: Ryōsaku Ogawa
Site area: 35,508 square feet
Building area: 373 square feet
Estimated cost: $2,780.00

AT LEAST two or three of the most clever architectural designs published each year in Japan are for diminutive country houses in the mountains or near the seashore. The reason must be that in designing small playhouses, architects feel free—or perhaps compelled—to give vent to fanciful ideas that in an ordinary city dwelling would be restrained by hard practicality.

The charming little pyramid shown here (§§113 & 115) stands in a deep forest in Tadeshina Heights, a mountainous area about a hundred miles northwest of Tokyo. The southward-sloping site affords an excellent view, and the designers have made the most of it by raising the house on stilts, these latter being formed by four massive logs resting on concrete foundations (§117).

The basic structure is a square box, to which cantilevered extensions have been added on all four sides. From each of the posts, four heavy braces extend upward, like the branches of a tree, to bolster long, double floor beams and, on the periphery of the building, the eaves purlins (§116). The central box is covered with a high hipped roof, which is lengthened on three sides to shelter the cantilevered projections. On the front side, where there is a balcony, the roof stops short, but the rafters extend to meet the supports from underneath (§118).

The interior is essentially a single space, but half of the eastern "wing" was partitioned off for a bathroom, and this helps to segregate the kitchen to some extent from the remainder of the room (§§119 & 120). On the south side a broad opening with sliding glass doors links the interior with the balcony (§114). The wooden shutters that cover the opening when the house is not in use are hinged at the top, and when raised, they form a sunshade for the balcony.

As the designers themselves have said of this house, the structure does not determine the space, and the space does not determine the structure, but the two fuse together to form a single entity. It should be added that the architects intended the house as an effort toward the creation of a design that could serve for prefabricated cottages of a similar nature.

◁ *§113 Though isolated at the time of this photograph, the house has since been joined by two others by the same designers. This view, which is from the southwest, shows the magnificent mountains in the background and the sweeping slope to the south.*

◁ *§114 The small raised tatami room on the right is the bedroom. In this photograph the glass doors between the living room and the balcony have been removed to give maximum openness on the south. Clerestory windows above the doors provide added light for the interior. The walls are set outside the four main posts, with the result that the latter are particularly emphatic.*

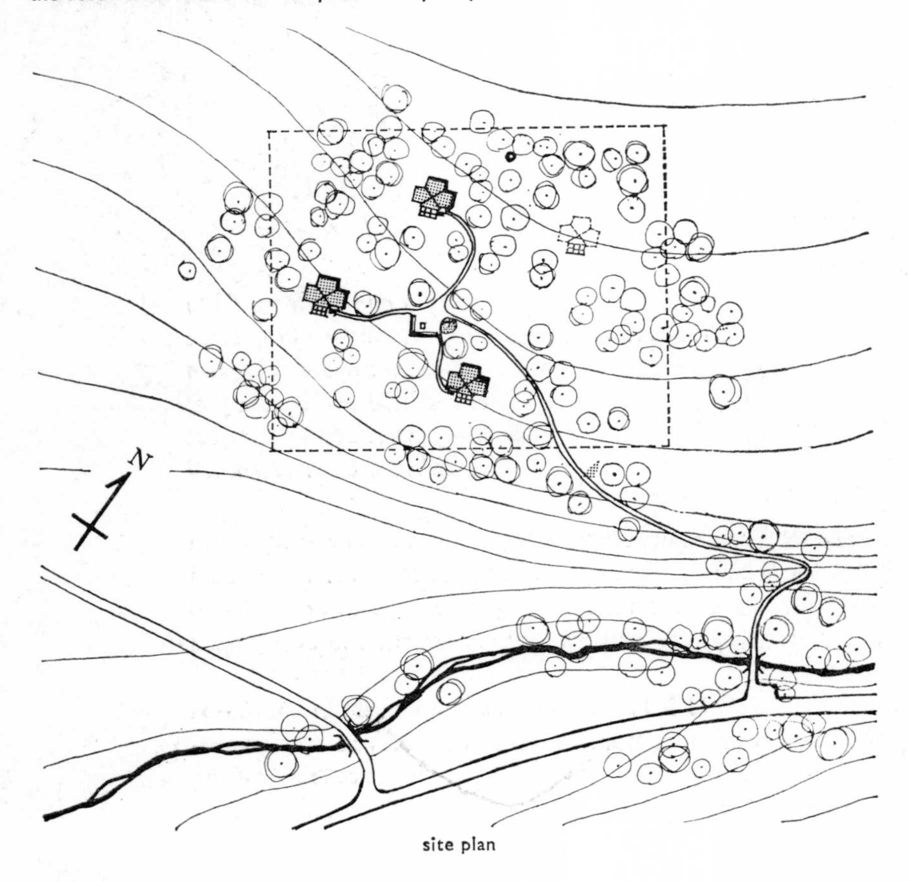

site plan

§115 The hipped roof has eaves reaching nearly to floor level on all sides save the south. Basically, the frame of the building is a square box with projections on all four sides. The south projection forms the open balcony, but the other three are integrated with the central living space. ▷

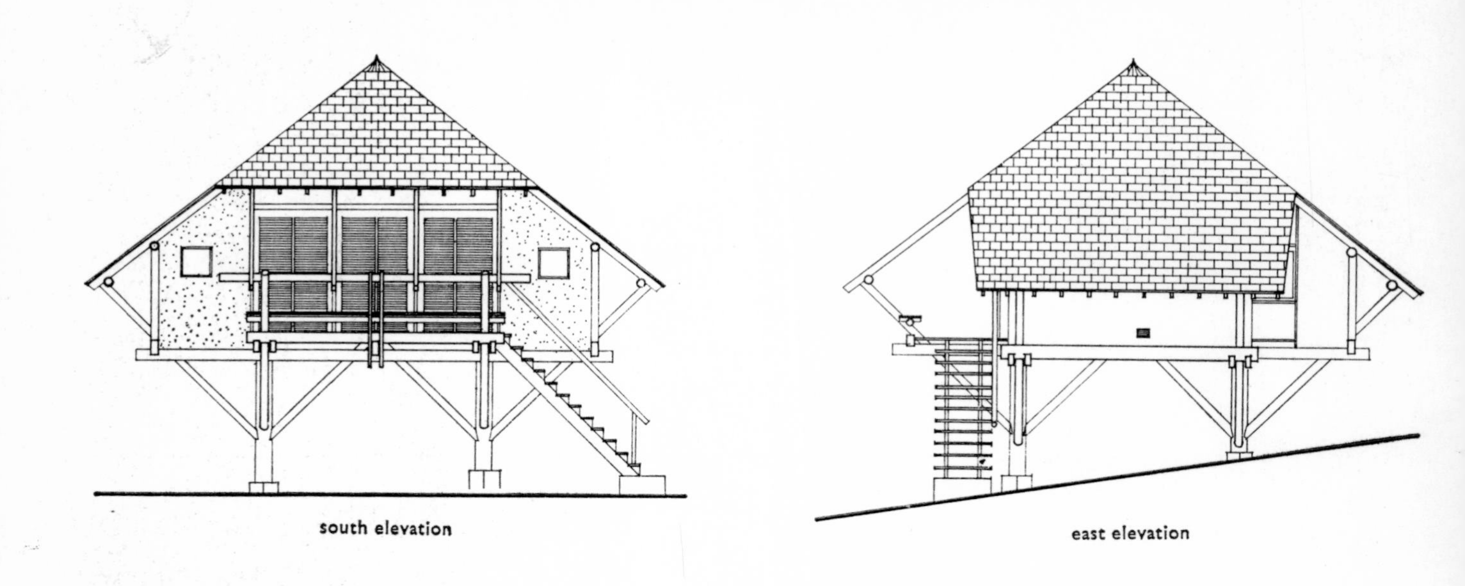

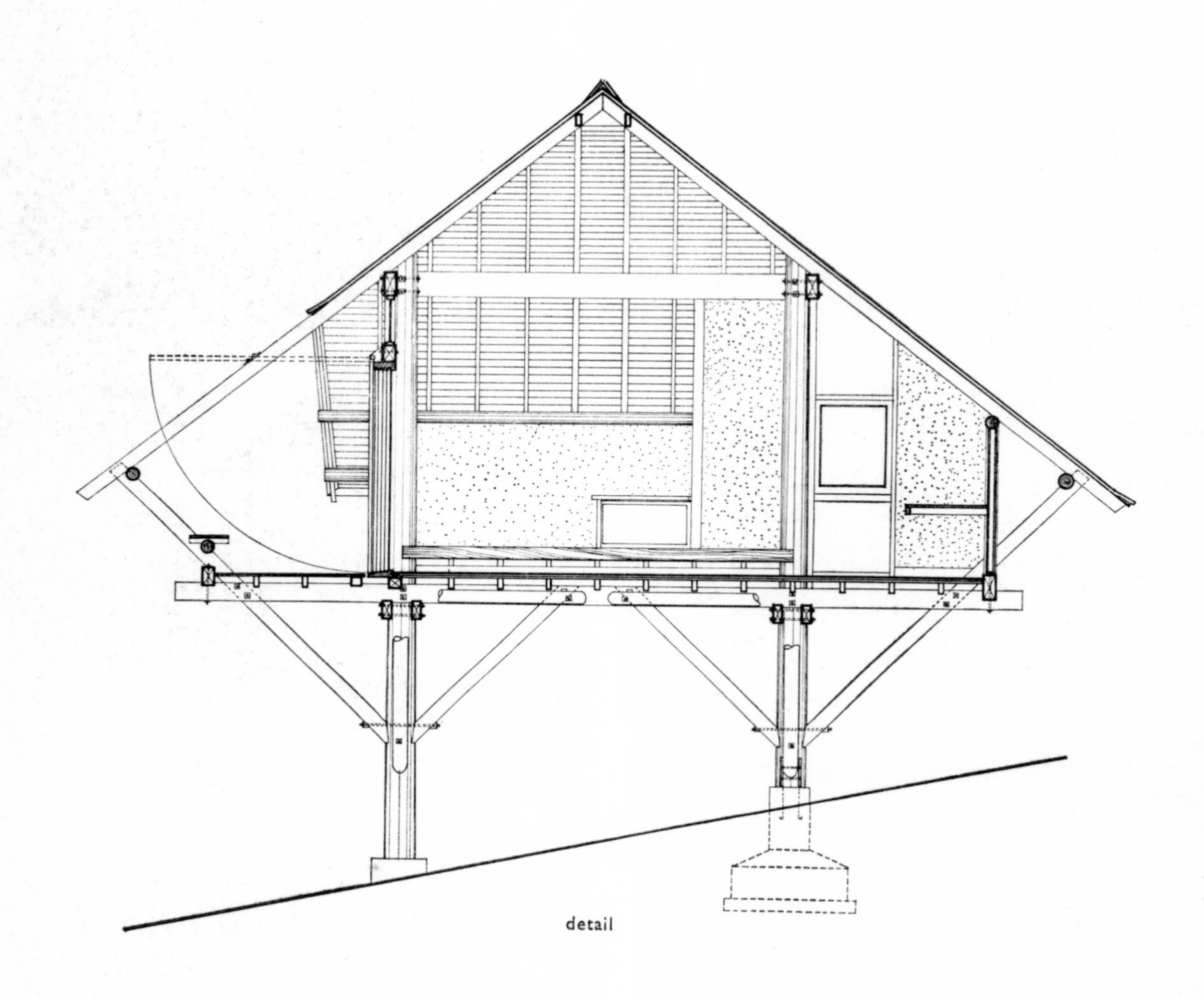

§116 The concrete foundations on which the four massive posts rest are sunk several feet into the ground. The roof is of wooden shingles. ▷

§118 Even on the south, where the eaves are shortened, rafters descend to meet the braces from below, thus completing the symmetry of the structure. Blinds hinged at the top serve as rain shutters when closed and as sunshades when open. Visible at the far right is a floor-level window in the tatami room.

◁ *§117 The posts are like four sturdy trees from which diagonal braces emerge like so many branches. The outer braces extend beyond the floor beams to meet the purlins at the outer edge of the roof. The structure is further strengthened by horizontal braces set diagonally across the four corners of the central area.*

§119 Under the eaves on the north side of the house are a built-in desk and a platform that serves as a sofa bed.

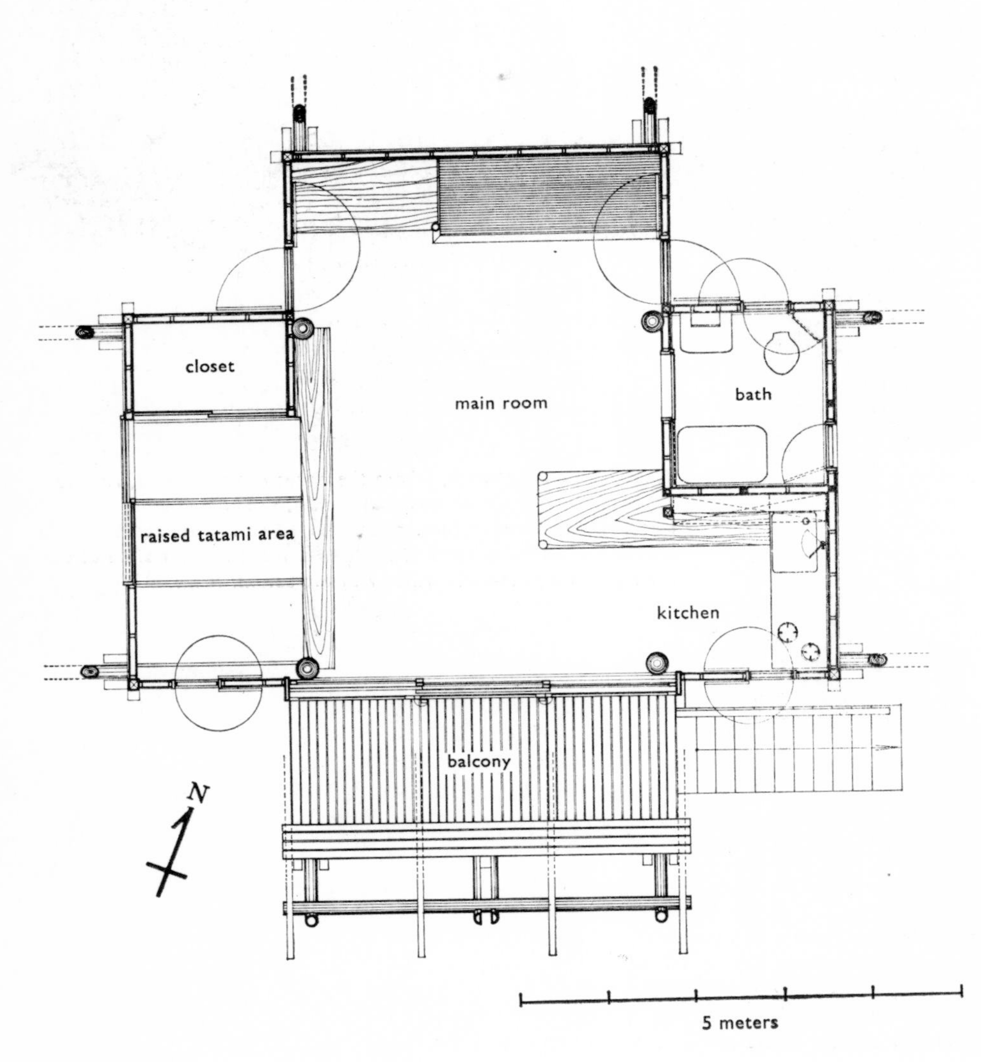

§120 The interior is a single space, except for the white walled-in section that contains the toilet and bath. This room performs the incidental function of isolating the kitchen somewhat from the remainder of the interior. The right side of the tabletop extends into the kitchen to form a work counter. ▷

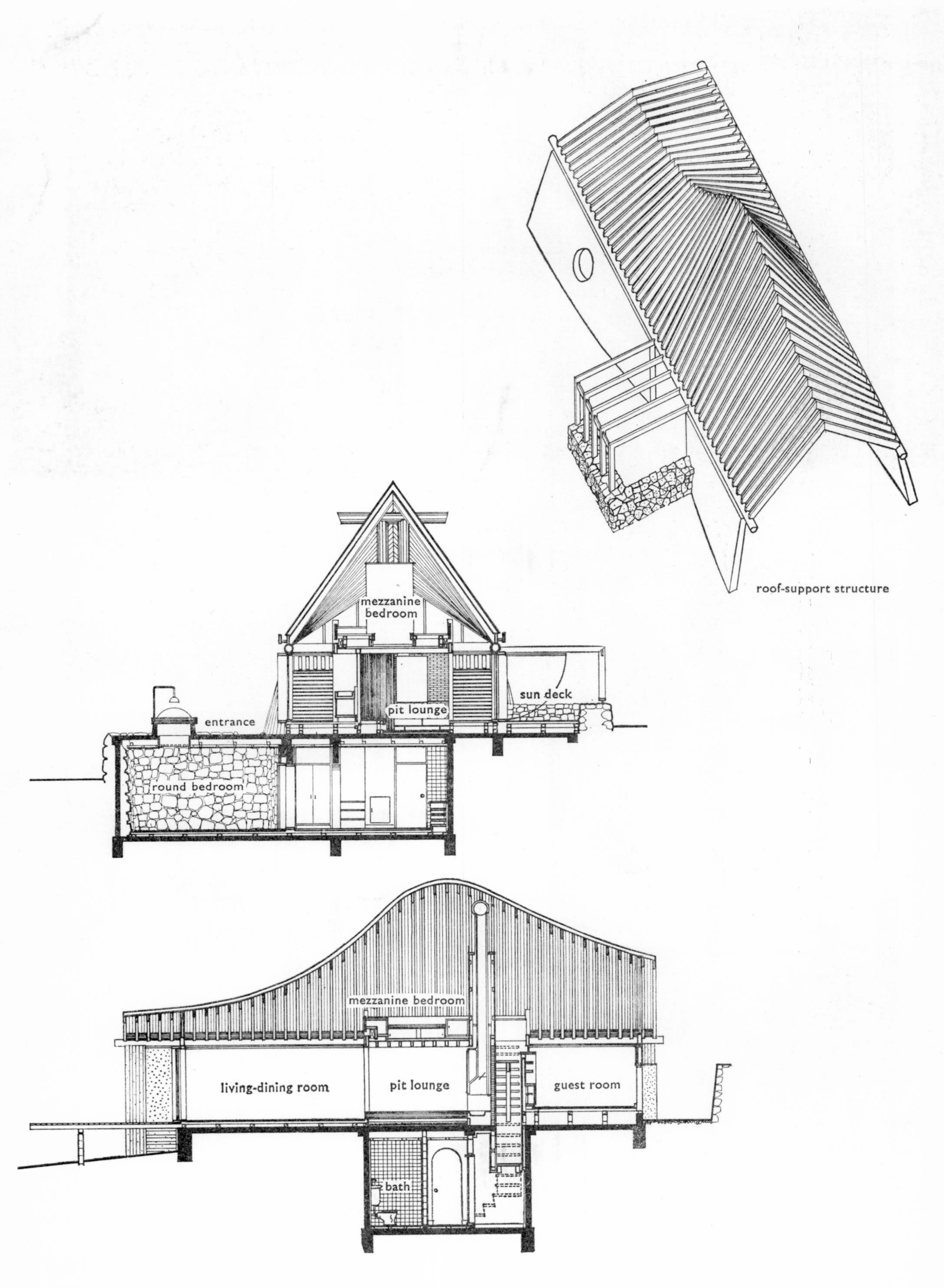
roof-support structure
mezzanine bedroom
sun deck
pit lounge
entrance
round bedroom
mezzanine bedroom
living-dining room
pit lounge
guest room
bath

THE HOUSE CALLED "MOBY DICK"

Architect: Dan Miyawaki
Location: Lake Yamanaka, Yamanashi Prefecture
Builders: Maki Construction Co.
Site area: 18,227 square feet
Building area: 836 square feet
Total floor area: 1,301 square feet
Estimated cost: $20,830.00

IT IS SAFE to assume that Captain Ahab, in all his wanderings, would never have thought to look for his quarry on the shores of Lake Yamanaka, smack in the middle of Japan, and the rest of us can be excused for suspecting at a glance that a building resembling a large white whale is likely to be a stunt of some sort. As it happens, however, the unusual shape of this "Moby Dick" was dictated largely by the severe weather conditions in the area where it is located and by the owner's wish to be able to use it all year round.

The site, which is in the western foothills of Mount Fuji, slopes down toward the lake, and in winter it is almost constantly swept by cold winds from the mountain. Zero temperatures and snow to a depth of three feet are not uncommon, and a cold heavy fog often covers the lake and its environs. In the summer, on the other hand, all this is changed, and the area becomes a favorite vacation resort for people fleeing from the heat of Tokyo. For winter, it was necessary to make as complete and secure a shelter as possible, but for summer, there had to be means of enjoying the cool breezes from the lake.

To satisfy the former condition, the designer employed a continuous roof that slopes up sharply at one end to accommodate a small mezzanine bedroom inside. To satisfy the latter, he provided a large opening and a sun deck facing on the lakeside (§123 & COLOR §15).

The unusual roof-support structure consists of about 100 rafters, each set at a different slope from the next. The rafters rest on round steel girders, which are in turn supported by concrete walls, curved to accord with the outward thrust of the roof. The designer is hardly exaggerating when he says that "aside from the floors, there are no straight lines in the building."

The owner of the house is a well-known designer of men's clothing, who customarily lives in a hotel in Tokyo, but who retreats to "Moby Dick" whenever he can find time, often with two or three guests. By integrating a straightforward floor plan with the curving roof, the architect has given him a variety of spaces ranging from open to almost completely closed. At one end of the scale is the living room opening on the sun deck (§123 & COLOR §16); at the other, a subterranean den whose only link with the exterior is a skylight (COLOR §17). In between are a reasonably spacious guest bedroom (§127), a low-ceilinged pit lounge with fireplace (§122), and the mezzanine bedroom, supported by amusing columns that double as lightposts. The bath and toilet are in the basement, adjacent to the den. The house is heated primarily by two oil furnaces, one in the basement and one on the first floor.

The ribs of the roof structure are merely treated with oil, and their natural color combines with white plaster walls to form a typically plain Japanese color scheme. The frame of the mezzanine section is of Japanese cypress, also with a natural finish, but the interior of this area is garnished with cloth in several bright colors. The owner cooperated with the architect in selecting the simple, but tasteful furnishings.

◁ *§121 A view from the south shows the white walls and curving profile that gained the house its name. The round bubble window provides light for the living room, as well as a view of Mount Fuji on the rare occasions when it is not hidden by clouds.*

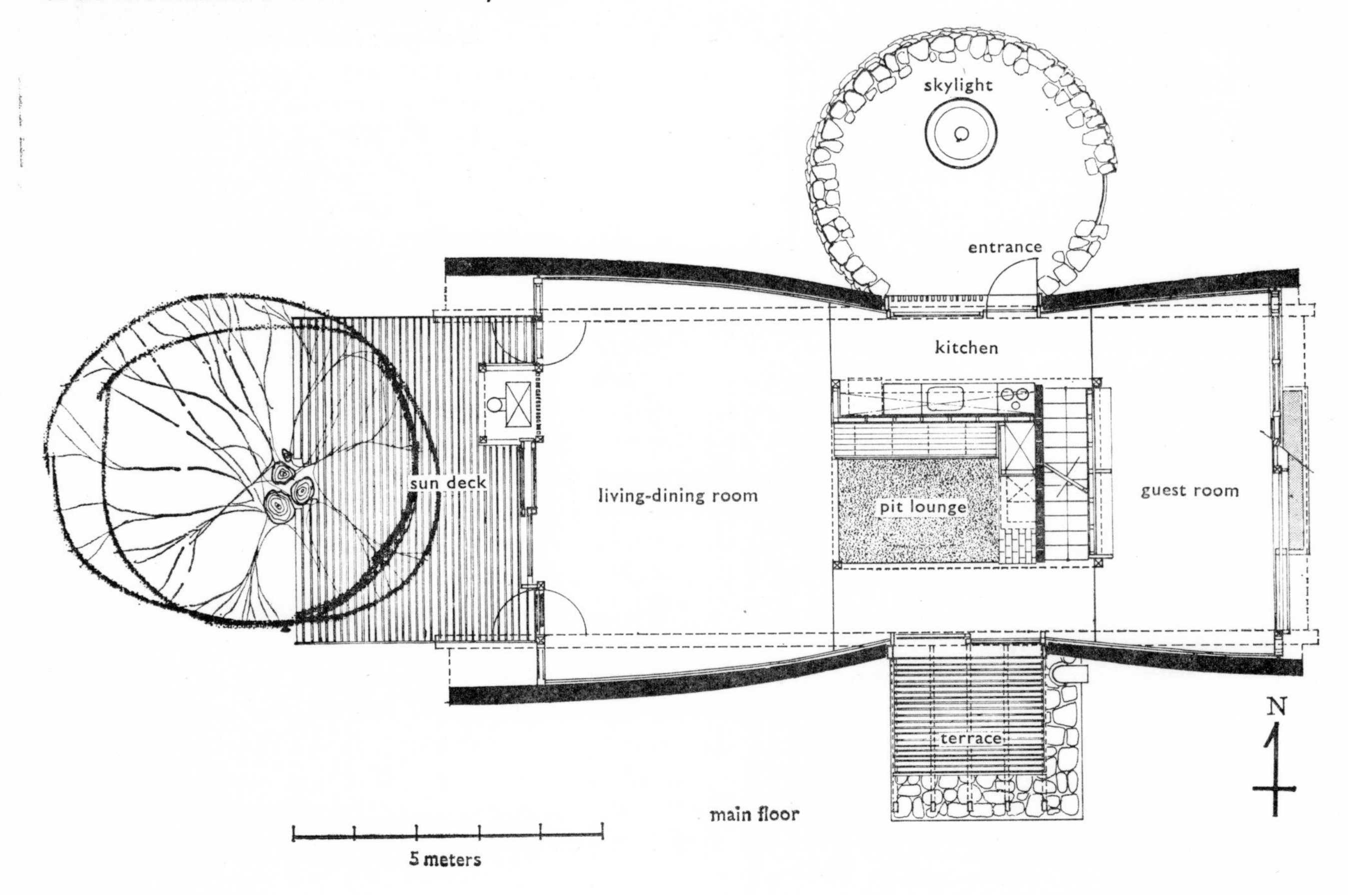

§122 A view from the living room toward the east shows the low-ceilinged pit with its open fireplace. The ribs of the roof structure thrust upward above this section to make room for the mezzanine bedroom, which is surrounded by only a railing.

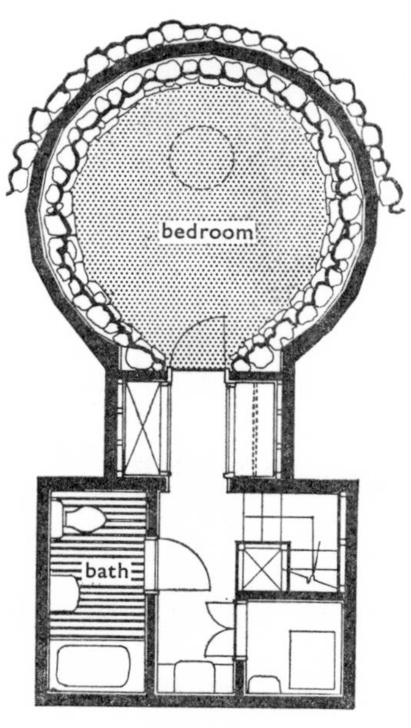

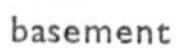

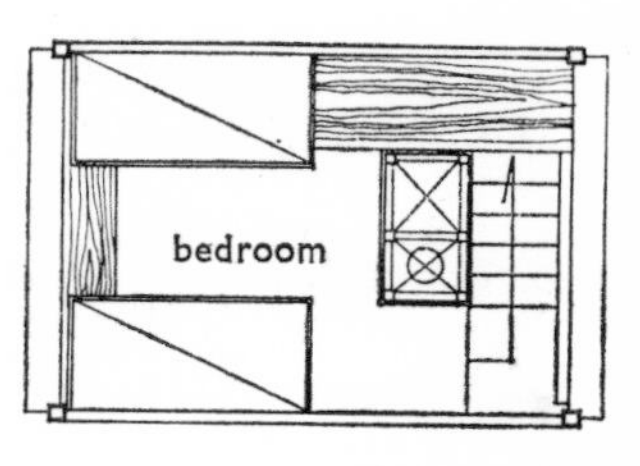

mezzanine

§123 The large opening on the west end of the living room looks out on Lake Yamanaka. Because of the severe winters in this district, glass doors and windows in the house all have double panes, and a variety of grilles and shutters provide further protection when necessary.

COLOR §15 *The walls and eaves extend to form a protective hood over the large lakeside opening, but there is a sun deck for use in the summer when the weather permits outdoor relaxation.*

§124 This photograph shows one of the round steel girders that support the ribs of the roof structure. At the corner of the dining area, a stand for flowers and ornaments has casually, but artfully been put together with bricks.

COLOR §16 *The color scheme as a whole is neutral, the dominant shade being the natural color of the wooden parts, but in the fireplace-pit area, there is a wide range of bright solid colors, varying with the function of the objects they adorn.*

§126 A terrace on the south side of the house is covered with a pergola and surrounded by a low stone wall, so that it gives one the feeling of being in a semi-enclosed room, rather than a projected outdoor space. ▷

§125 From the central sector of the house the walls curve outward horizontally, while slanting in vertically. Whereas most Japanese houses are made up almost entirely of straight lines and rectangular planes, the emphasis in "Moby Dick" is on curves.

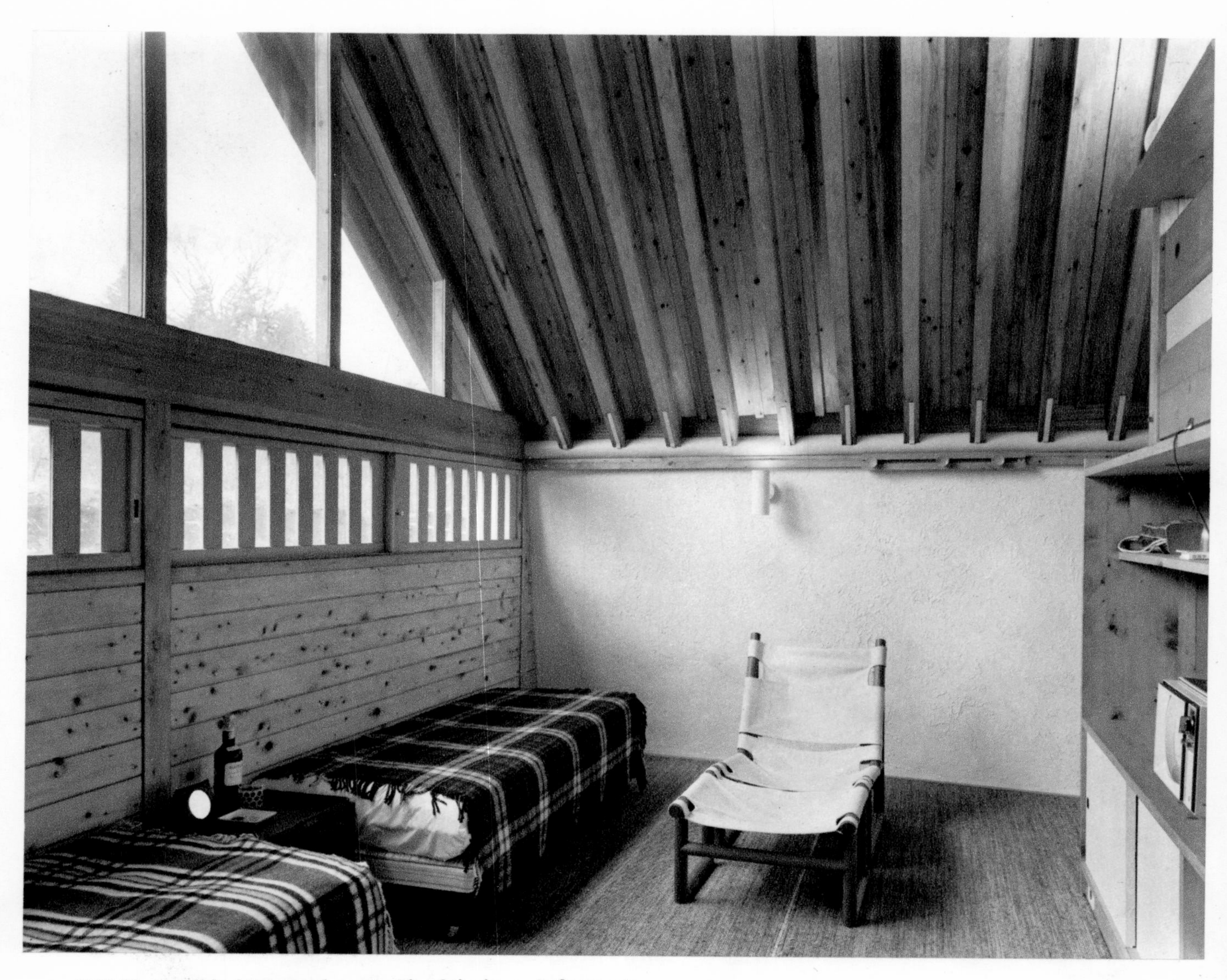

§127 The small bedroom on the east side of the house is for guests. Since the road is on this side, the room has only small openings at eye level and is lighted primarily by large clerestory windows. At the extreme upper right is the railing of the stairway to the upstairs bedroom.

COLOR §17 *Perhaps to balance the square, unwalled bedroom above the fireplace pit, there is a round, windowless bedroom, walled with stone, in the basement. The skylight has a weather-proof plastic dome, above which there is an outside light.*

§128 A night view shows the large trees on the lakeside and the hoodlike shelter over the living room silhouetted against the sky. ▷

VARIATION ON THE CLASSIC STYLE

Architect: Nobuko Nakahara
Location: Moroyama, Saitama Prefecture
Builders: Miyoshi Construction Co.
Site area: 18,292 square feet
Building area: 1,762 square feet
Floor area: 1,316 square feet
Estimated cost: $23,610.00

"I THINK," writes the lady architect who designed this house, "that a house has to be able to take a lot of rough use to be comfortable. There is not much pleasure if you have to be on your toes all the time for fear you might damage something. In this house, the dynamic space created by the big beams, the interior atmosphere dominated by natural wood, and the exposed bolts all work together to create a forcefulness that will stand up against rough treatment." And so they do, although the exterior has the graceful sloping lines and deep eaves that characterize many classical Japanese houses (§§130 & 131).

The building is essentially a weekend house in the mountains, but it also serves as a permanent dwelling for the owner's invalid child. Consequently, the plan is composed of two parts, one containing the basic spaces needed by the child and his nurse (or at times one of the parents) and another containing rooms that are used only occasionally. When not occupied, these latter rooms are closed off from the outside with wooden rain shutters, but small transom windows above the shutters make it possible to air them without actually opening them.

The basic structure creates a single large space, in which the underside of the roof forms the ceiling (§133). Contrary to the usual practice, the partitioning of the rooms does not necessarily follow the lines of the structure (§132). The interior space derives much of its strength, as well as its accent, from bold diagonal beams, sheathed with slanting planks that run up to the roof.

The house is backed on the north by a cliff, and there are mountains on all sides save the east, where the ground slopes down toward the Kanto Plain. The living room and child's room have large openings both on this side and on the sunny south side. A spacious deck runs around three sides of the building at a level somewhat lower than that of the interior floors (§133). The deck railing is formed by heavy logs, which cross each other at the corners in a fashion that is traditional, but more vigorous than is customary in traditional buildings.

The room described in the plans as the "dining room" is more on the order of an informal sitting room, centering around a pit fireplace with a chimney hood. On the north side of the house and somewhat isolated from the remainder of it is a tearoom to which the owner's wife likes to retire from time to time for a moment of solitude and rest.

◁ *§129 A view from the southeast shows the large openings on the south and southeast sides of the house. The corner room with shoji closed is occupied by the owner's invalid son, and the room at the center with shoji open is the living room. At the far left is the Japanese-style bedroom.*

§130 The gently sloping hipped roof and strong horizontal lines of the floor, railing, and eaves brings to mind a style of Buddhist architecture called Karayō, which flourished briefly in the late twelfth and thirteenth centuries, but the resemblance is probably coincidental. The photograph was taken from the east, which is the only direction in which the ground slopes downward. ▷

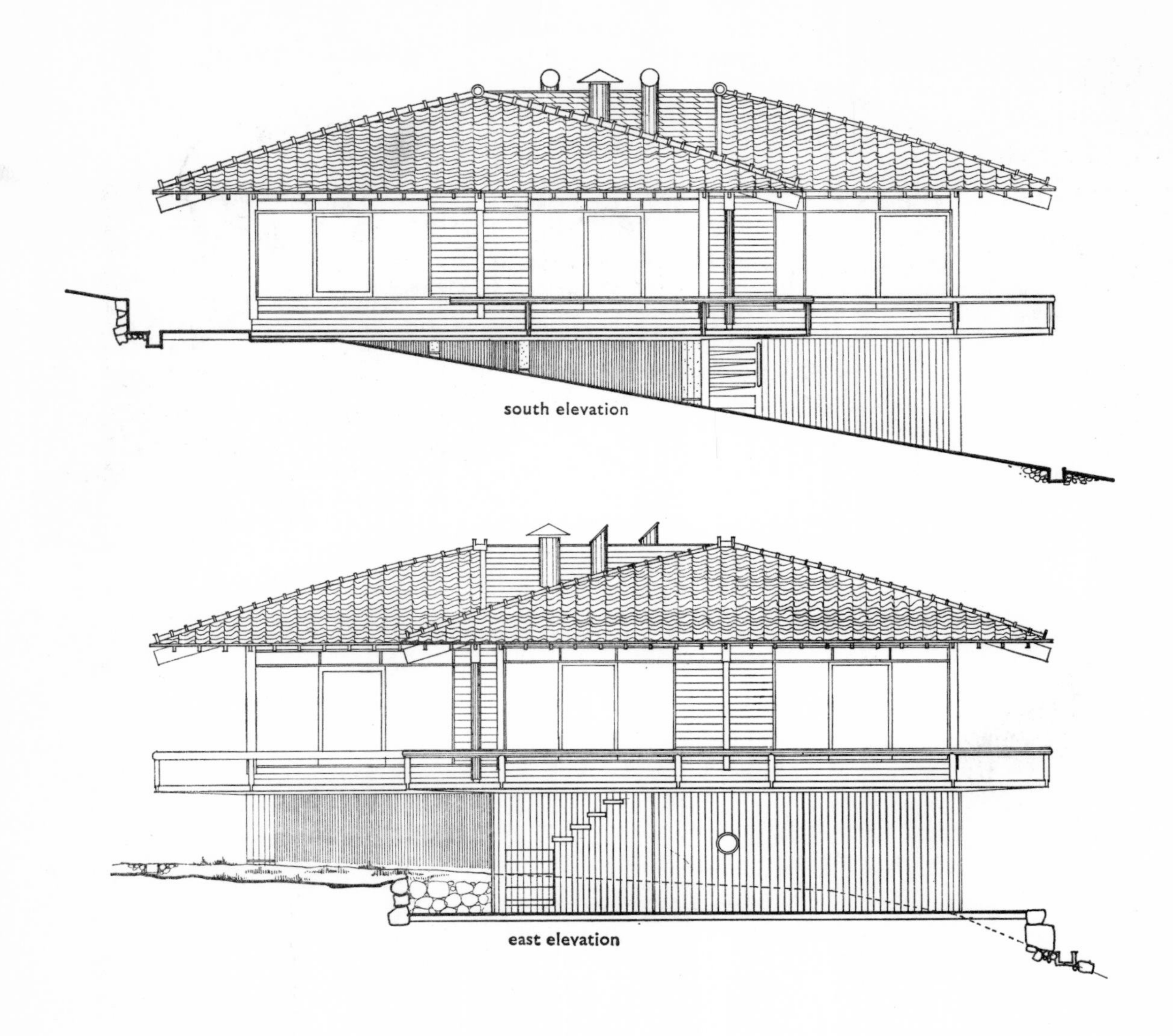
south elevation
east elevation

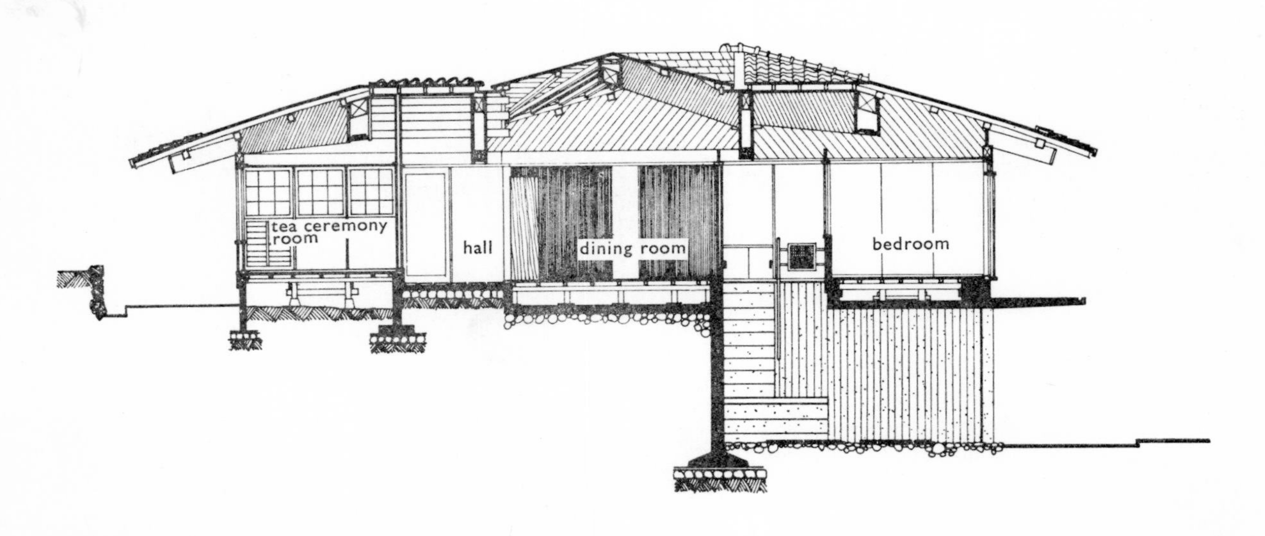
tea ceremony room
hall
dining room
bedroom

§131 The veranda has been dropped about a foot below floor level, and rain shutters (in the wooden casings between the windows), usually flush with the doors at the bottom, are brought down to veranda level, thus avoiding leakage of water under the shutters—a common failing in Japanese houses.

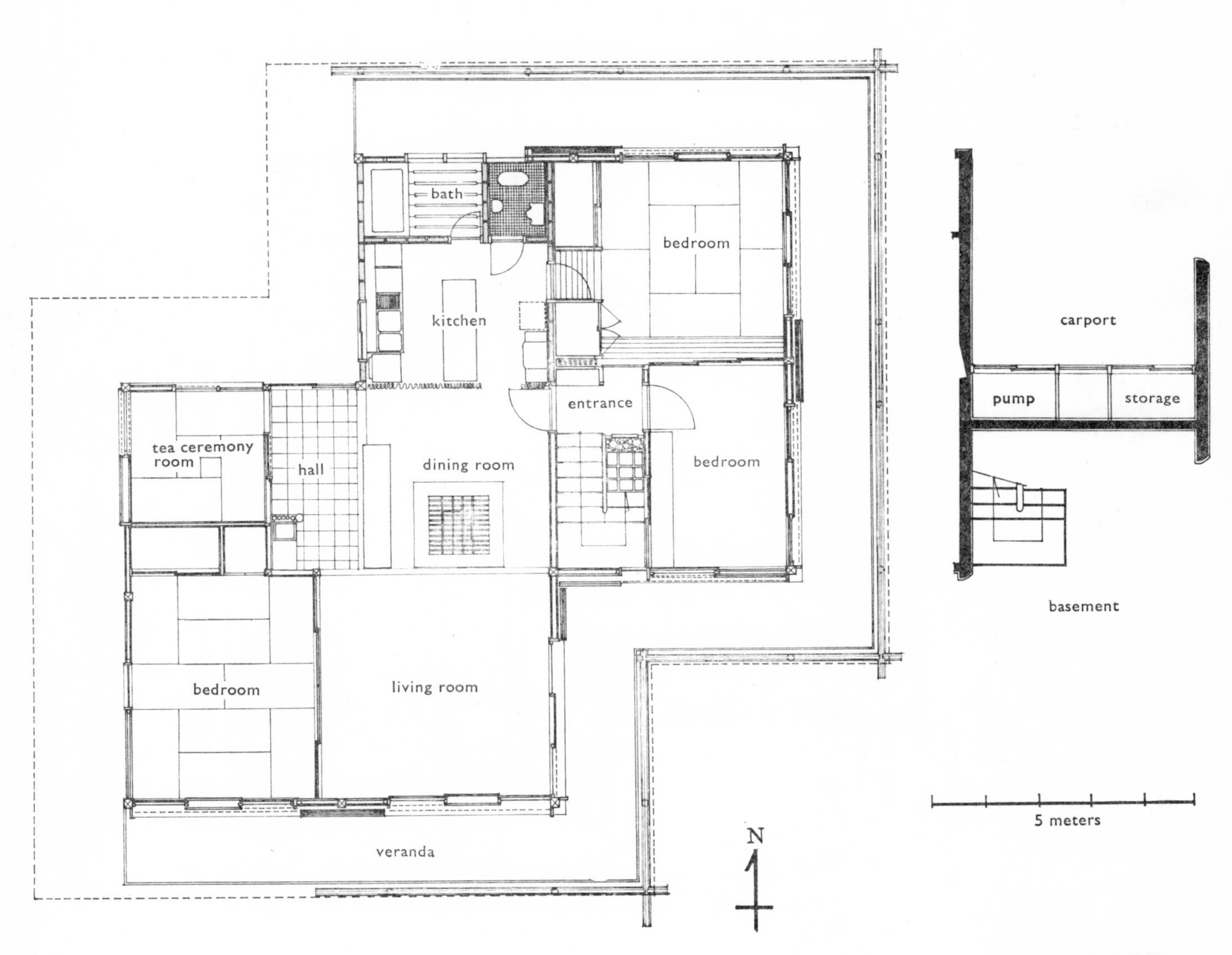

§133 The dining room is a kind of indoor barbecue, which can also be used simply as a place to gather around the fire in the winter. In the background is the living room, and to the right, behind the cupboard, the kitchen.

§132 An impressive feature of the structure is the treatment of the beams, which are sheafed up to the roof with diagonal boarding. As can be seen at the right, the interior partitioning is independent of the main structure. Transom windows above the doors and rain shutters permit airing even when the outside shutters are closed.

§134 Even the quiet bedroom space is sliced diagonally by one of the beams of the main structure.

§135 The railings of the veranda, which runs around three sides of the house, overlap at the corners as in ancient buildings.

SPLIT-LEVEL COUNTRY HOUSE

Architects: Design Department, Kajima Construction Co.
Location: Karuizawa, Nagano Prefecture
Builders: Maebashi Office, Kajima Construction Co.
Site area: 162,180 square feet
Building area: 2,927 square feet
Total floor area: 4,320 square feet
Estimated cost: Not obtainable

THE PLAN FOR this house comprises five square sectors which are set at five different levels, but which overlap neatly in the central part of the building. At the lowest level, on the north, is the servants' section, which contains three bedrooms and a bath. Up a few steps from this, on the west, are the kitchen and dining room (§141), and at a slightly higher level, on the south, is the main living room. On the east and at the same level as the living room is a large entrance hall (§139), from which a stairway leads up half a floor to a suite for the owner's children. This is directly above the servants' quarters. Still another stairway leads from a hall in the children's suite up another half-flight to the master bedroom section, which is above the dining-kitchen area. Lines of movement are excellent; a central fireplace forms a nucleus for a sort of spiral that starts in the lowest part of the house and continues up and around to the master bedroom at the top level.

The house was built for the president of a large company, who often entertains here, and whose guests are likely to vary from those whom he barely knows to his most intimate friends. The plan is accordingly arranged so that some callers can be received in the large entrance hall and entertained in the high-ceilinged formal living room, without penetrating farther into the house. More intimate callers can be invited into the dining room sector, where there is a second, more informal, living room by the central fireplace (§143).

The spatial variation in the more public section of the house is noteworthy. Both the entrance hall and the main living room are open upward to the second-floor ceiling, but the more private living room and dining room have ceilings of normal height. The eastern half of the master bedroom forms an overhang, with windows opening on the entrance hall and the living room below. There are box gardens with ferns and vines at three levels in the entrance hall, and a fourth box garden hangs below the master-bedroom windows on the living room side (§142).

The wooded setting of the house is quiet and restful, and the designers have attempted to make each window in the building a picture window, with its own distinctive view—a task made simpler by the many changes in floor level. The living room has, in addition to broad glass doors on the south side, a large clerestory window that furnishes light to the whole south side of the interior, including the master bedroom on the second floor (§140).

One of the nuisances about country houses in Japan is that of opening and closing the house on arrival and departure. The openings are normally covered with sliding wooden shutters, which are apt to expand and contract with changes in the weather and thus to become very difficult to move. In a house as large as this, shutters of this kind would mean a good deal of time and effort in opening and closing, and the designers therefore chose to replace them with slide-away doors on railings inside the house. The purpose being not so much to protect the doors and windows as to keep the elements (and burglars) out of the interior, this arrangement is quite satisfactory.

◁ COLOR *§18 Seen on the south side of the house are a sun deck with a tree rising through it and the high windows of the main living room. To the left are the dining room on the first floor and the master bedroom on the second.*

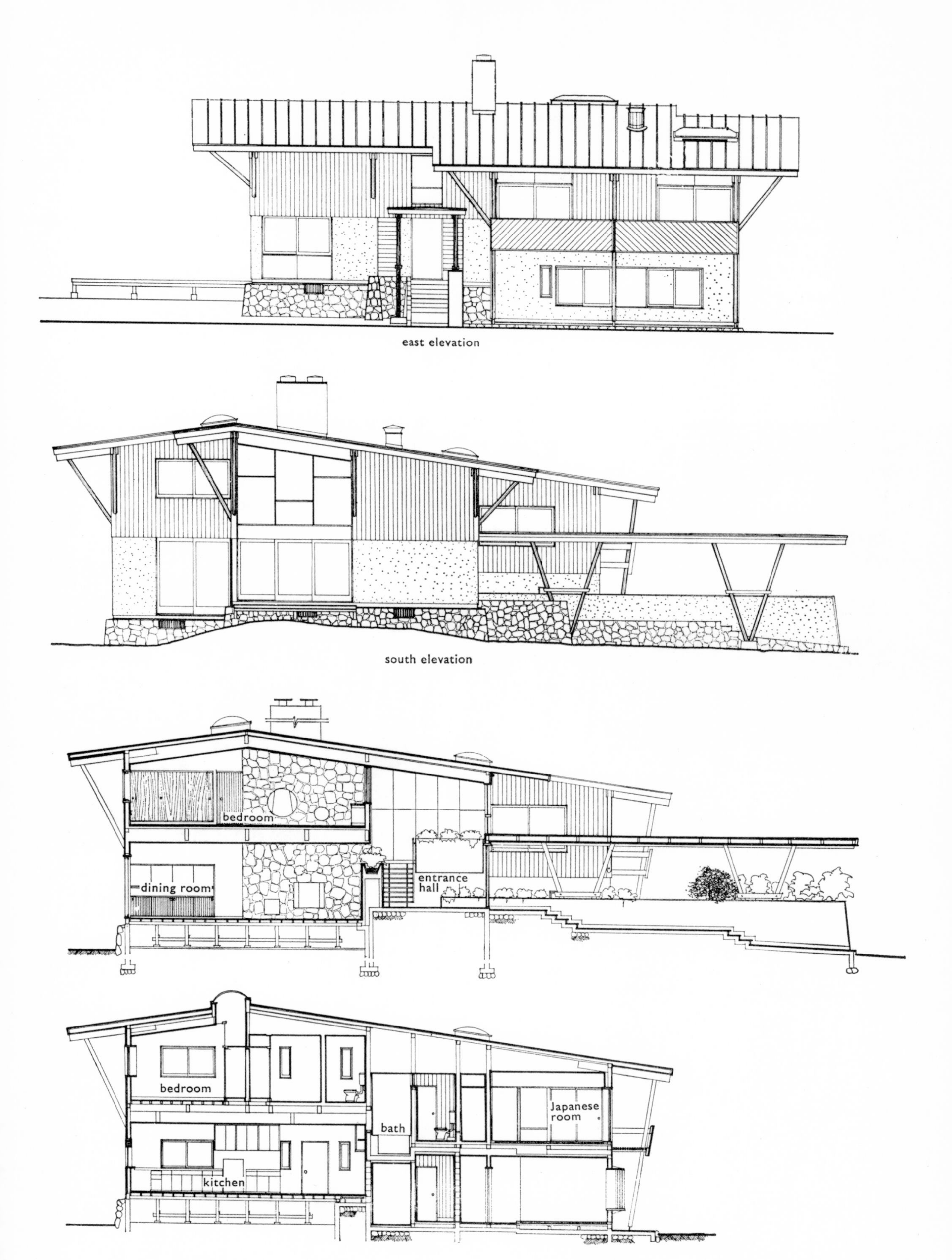
east elevation
south elevation
bedroom
dining room
entrance
hall
bedroom
bath
Japanese
room
kitchen

§136 Narrow vertical windows in the west walls of the dining room (left) and the living room furnish a certain amount of light even though the house is basically closed to the western sun. The long eaves, necessitated by frequent rainfall, are supported by braces rising diagonally from the main posts.

§137 The house is approached through a long covered passageway bordered on the right side by a series of box gardens. Not only the box gardens, but the brick-tile paving are continued in the entrance hall. At the right are the servants' quarters on the lower floor and the children's suite on the upper.

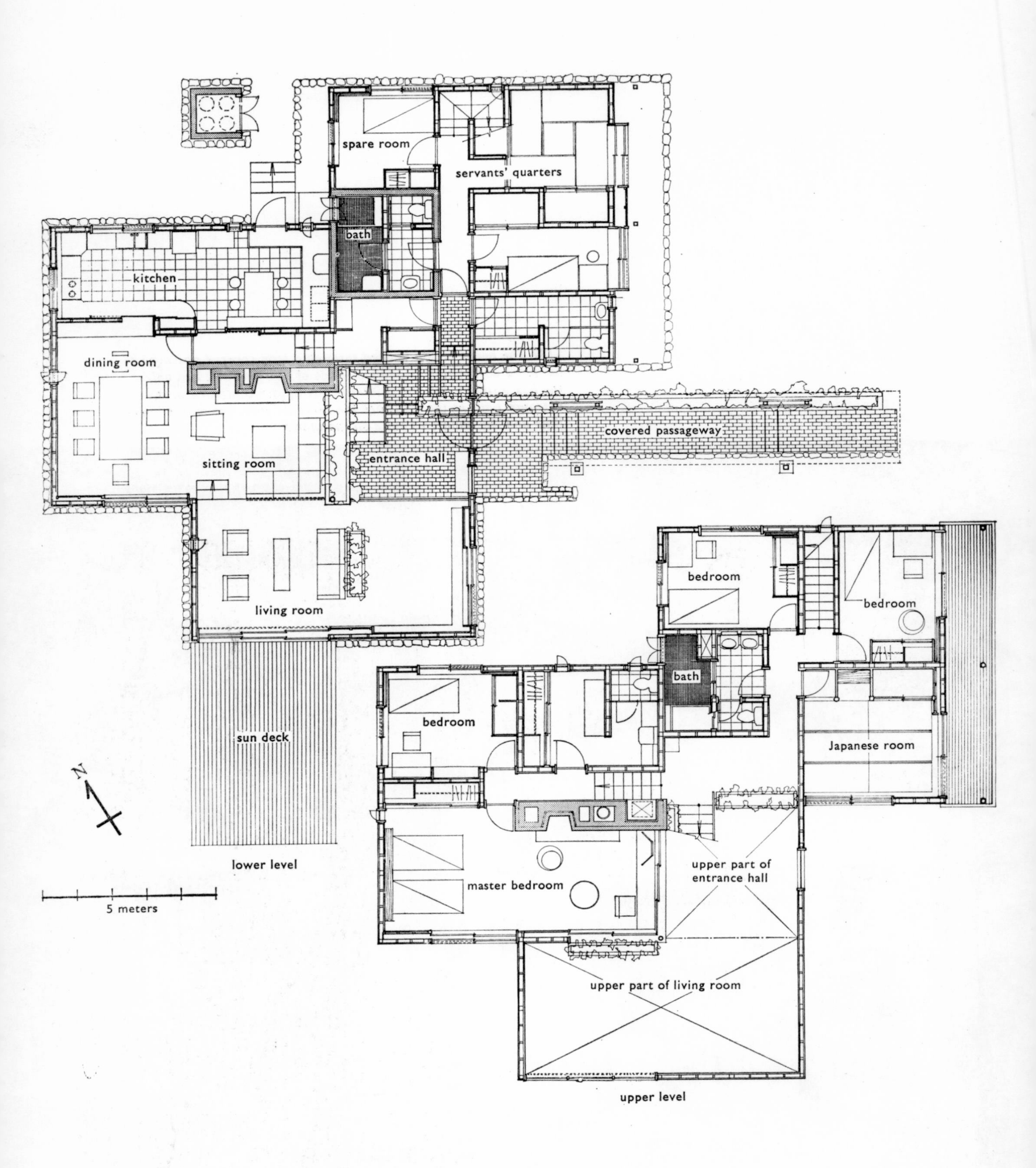

spare room
servants' quarters
bath
kitchen
dining room
sitting room
entrance hall
covered passageway
living room
sun deck
lower level
N
5 meters
bedroom
bedroom
bath
bedroom
Japanese room
master bedroom
upper part of
entrance hall
upper part of living room
upper level

§138 A view from the entrance hall shows the flower boxes along the covered approach from the driveway. The V-shaped roof supports are appropriately rustic.

§140 A high clerestory window on the south side of the living room provides light not only for that room, but also for the east half of the second-floor master bedroom, which has windows opening on the living room. ▷

§139 The large entrance hall, like the living room, is open to the second-floor ceiling. The stairway at the left leads to the master bedroom (overhang) and the children's suite, and the stairs at the lower center lead to the servants' quarters. The main entrance is on the right.

§142 The walls in the living room and in much of the house are ▷ of knotty pine, as is appropriate for a house in this peaceful wooded setting. The flower box at the upper right hangs from the window ledge of the master bedroom.

§141 A blind forms a partial visual barrier between the main living room and the more informal sitting room adjacent to the dining area.

§143 At the left is the inner living room, where furniture is gathered around a large stone fireplace and hearth.

CLIFF HOUSE BY THE SEA

Architect: Masako Hayashi
Location: Itō, Shizuoka Prefecture
Builders: Satō Construction Co.
Site area: 71,016 square feet
Building area: 1,151 square feet
Total floor area: 2,066 square feet
Estimated cost: $24,580.00

THE IZU PENINSULA, about 70 miles southwest of Tokyo, is one of the city's favorite playgrounds, and deservedly so, since it offers not only innumerable hot-spring resorts, but a stunning coastline, a warm climate, and, in the mountainous interior, clear streams where the brook trout are abundant. The house shown here stands near the end of a rocky promontory on the east coast of the peninsula, in a spot that has not only fine old pine trees, but a splendid view of the Pacific Ocean and, below the cliff, a small sandy beach.

The building was actually designed as a weekend lodge for five or six couples living in Tokyo, but with only minor adjustments it would be an excellent single-family residence.

The designer, one of Japan's leading women architects, is noted for the vigor of her structures and forms. Here, slanting log posts bigger than telephone poles are linked together with large double beams to form a bold A-frame structure, and the gables are made to flare out stylishly toward the top, in a fashion reminiscent of prehistorical Japanese houses (§145 & COLOR). Inside, the structure is exposed, and the ceiling is formed by the underside of the roof. For added visual strength, the large boards that line the roof are placed diagonally. All wooden parts have a natural finish (COLOR §19).

The interior spaces were set at a number of different levels, so as to allow high ceilings where they were needed and to achieve maximum openness and spatial variation within the limits of the normally somewhat confining A-shaped structure. On the first floor, a ground-level area paved with natural stone contains the toilet and baths, together with a storage space for swimming and water-skiing gear (§149). Raised slightly above this, but still at first-floor level, are the living room (§§146 & 147), which is open to the peak of the roof, and three bedrooms with ceilings of normal height (§150). Adjacent to the living room, but a half-floor higher, is a small parlor that doubles as an entrance hall. A short flight of stairs at the inner end of this room leads to the second floor, which contains kitchen, dining room, and two small bedrooms. There being no wall on the west side of the dining room, this room overlooks the living room and entrance-parlor and receives much of its light from a large window under the gable at the west end of the house (§148). This window is echoed in reverse at the other end of the building, in a small third-floor bedroom overlooking the dining room.

On the seaward side of the building, which is to the south, a deck runs the length of the house (§§144 & 152), providing porch space not only for the living room, but for two of the first-floor bedrooms. The visual effect here of the sturdy posts and beams in juxtaposition with trees and rocks and sea is superb.

◁ *§144 On the south the posts of the "A" frame rest on massive concrete foundations. Rooms opening on the sun deck are the living room (left) and two bedrooms. A cutback in the middle section of the roof makes way for floor-level windows in the dining room on the second floor.*

§145 A view from the east shows the dramatic outward flare of the gable, as well as the stylish play of triangular wall and window at the third-floor level. Visible at the lower left is a section of Izu Peninsula's mountainous coastline. ▷

§146 The living room is seen here from the dining room on the second floor. At the right, on a level between the living and dining rooms, is an entrance hall that doubles as a small parlor.

COLOR §19 *A view from the entrance hall reveals the full boldness of the structure and the effective interplay of interior spaces. Under a single great shelter, rooms have been fitted in at various levels so that their ceilings are of heights appropriate to their particular functions.*

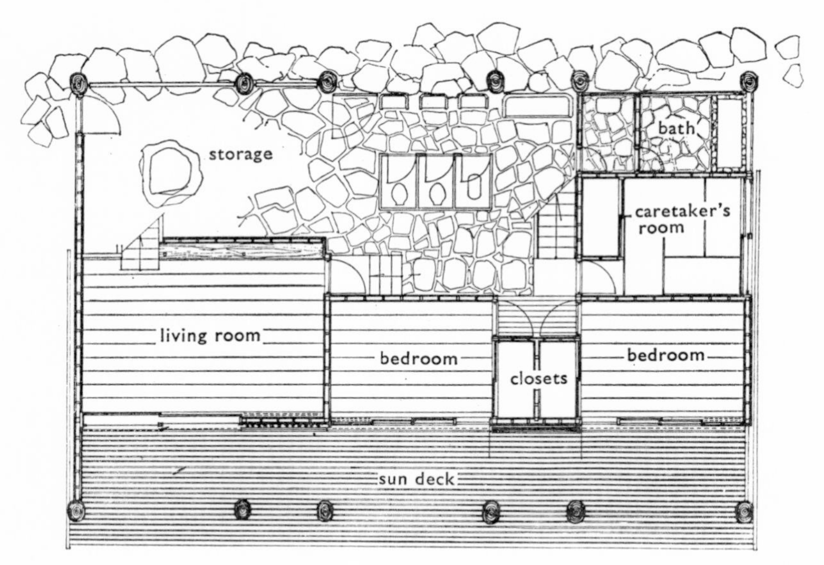
storage
bath
caretaker's room
living room
bedroom
closets
bedroom
sun deck

first floor

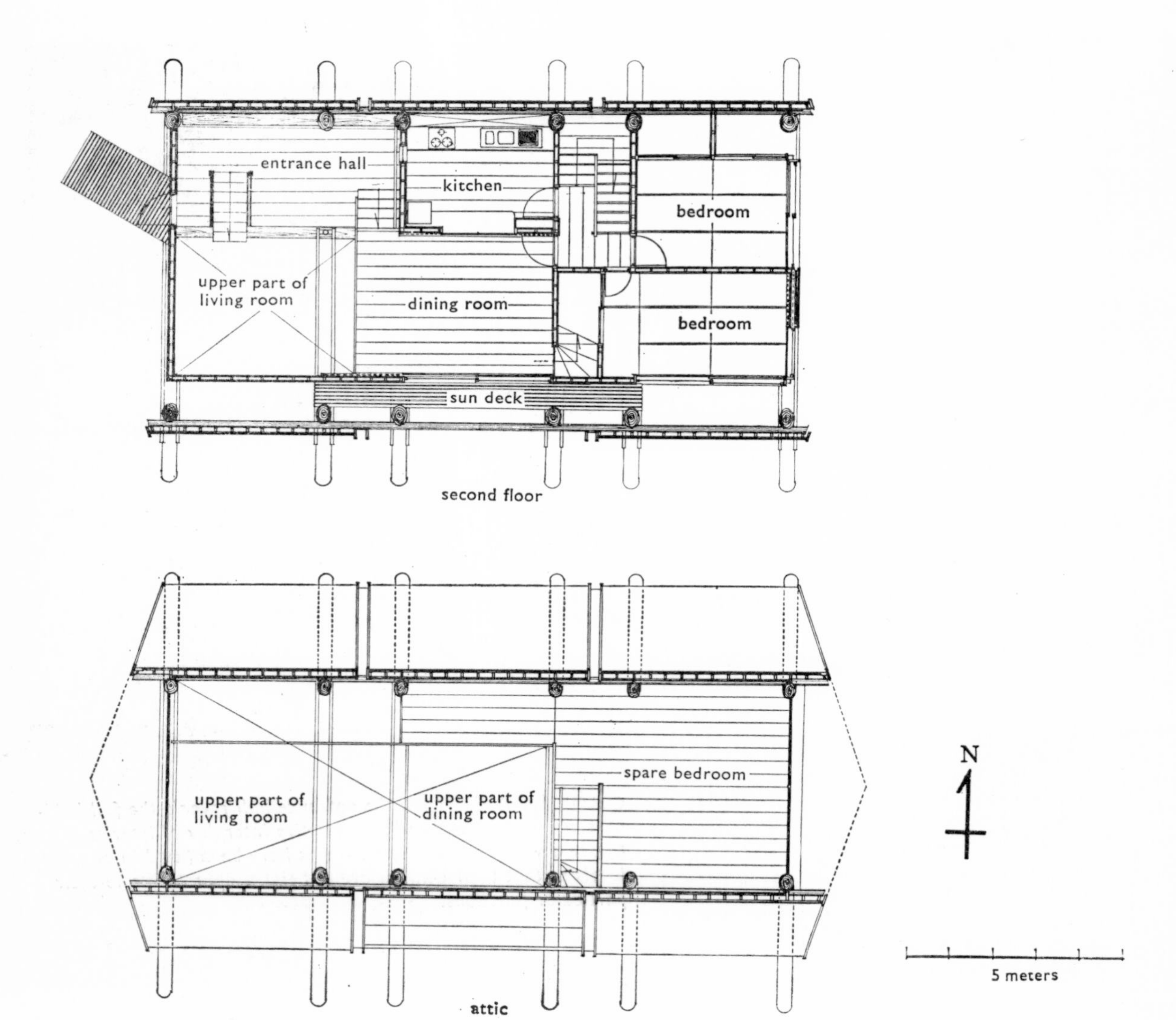
entrance hall
kitchen
bedroom
upper part of living room
dining room
bedroom
sun deck
second floor
upper part of living room
upper part of dining room
spare bedroom
attic
N
5 meters

§147 The living room has an excellent view of the coast to the southwest. As in most of the rest of the house, the walls here are of cryptomeria wood, polished with oil.

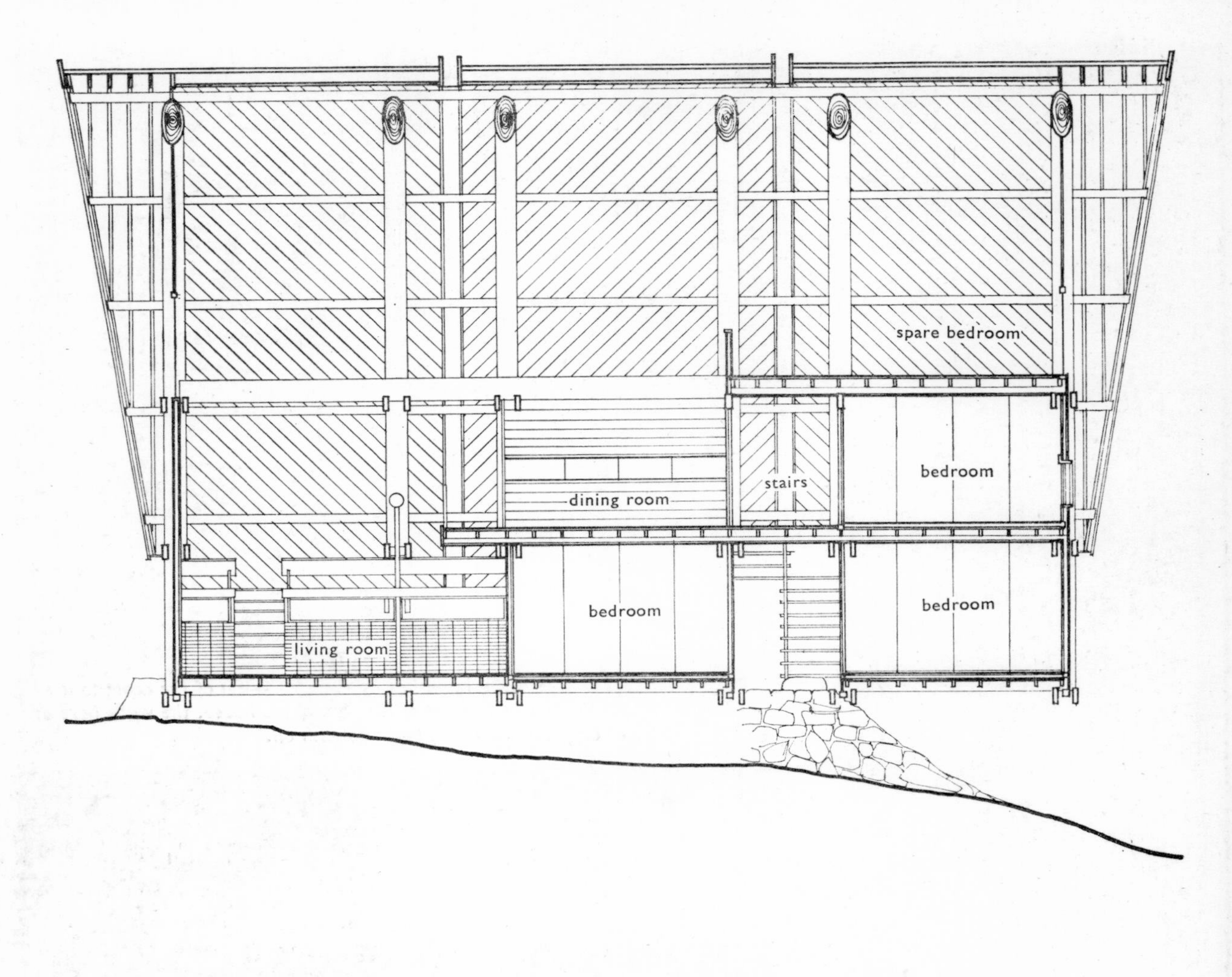

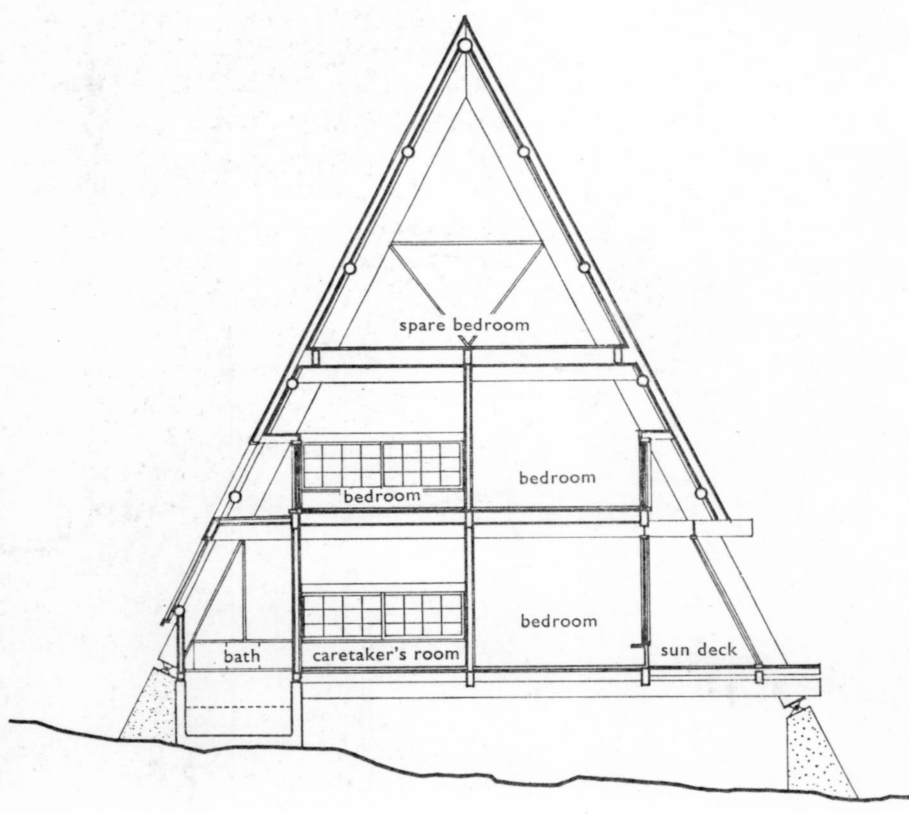

§148 At the west end of the house a clerestory window is segmented by an inverted triangular panel. At the east end, where there is a small bedroom at the same level, glass and wall panels are set in the same pattern, but reversed (see §145). ▹

◁ *§149 The north side of the first floor, which is paved with rough stones, contains the toilet and bath (extreme right), as well as a storage space for fishing equipment, water skis, and the like. The door in the center leads to the living room, and one of the two first-floor bedrooms is visible at the left.*

§150 The upper panes of the windows in the first-floor bedroom are fixed, but the smaller ones below can be opened for ventilation.

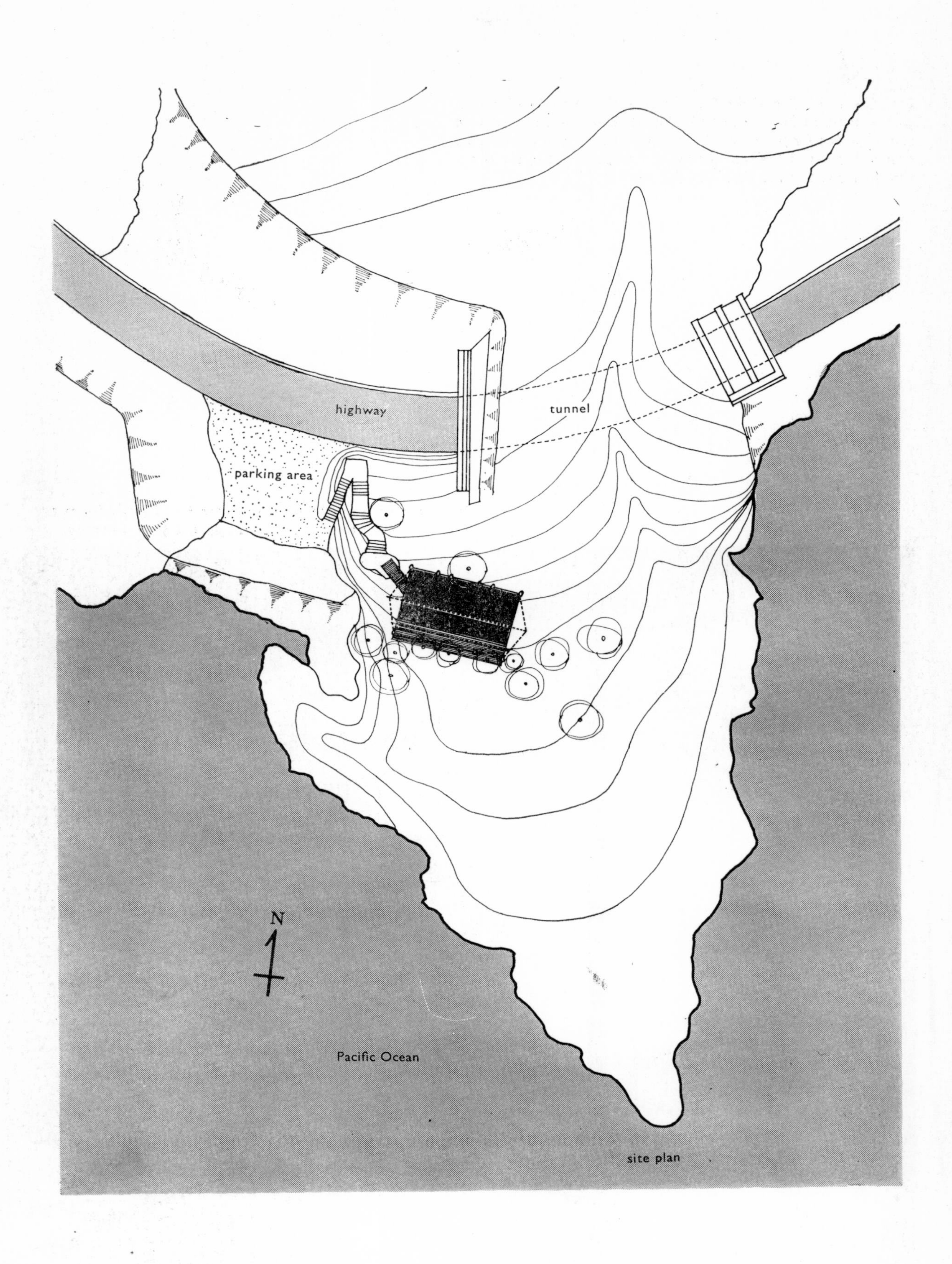

§151 A night view from above shows the sun deck on the south of the house and the waist-high windows of the dining room on the second floor. Huge diagonal posts and double beams frame the sun deck, which has a 180-degree view of the Pacific Ocean. ▷

§152 A late evening view with the interior lighted emphasizes the openness of the lower floor. The strips running up the roof are skylights.

Photographs appearing in this book have been made available through the courtesy of: Minoru Akiyama, §§ 19–26 and COLOR § 4; Chuokoron-sha, § 29; Akio Kawasumi, §§ 57–62, 136–143 and COLOR §§ 5, 9, 18; Akihisa Masuda, §§ 41–43, 45 and COLOR § 7; Osamu Murai, Cover, §§ 27–28, 30–35, 37, 39–40, 50–56, 63, 66–70, 78–79, 83, 121, 123–126, 128, 144–152 and COLOR §§ 6, 8, 10, 15–17, 19–20; Takashi Oyama, §§ 2, 4, 6, 9, 36, 38, 77, 80–82, 107–108; Yoshikatsu Saeki, §§ 10–18 and COLOR § 3; Kuniharu Sakumoto, §§ 71–76 and COLOR § 11; Shiro Seki, §§ 98–104 and COLOR § 13; Shinkenchiku-sha, §§ 64–65, 91–97, 105–106, 109–112, 122, 127 and COLOR §§ 12, 14; Shokokusha, §§ 44, 46–49, 113–120, 129–135; Toshio Taira, §§ 1, 3, 5, 7–8, 84–90 and COLOR §§ 1–2.

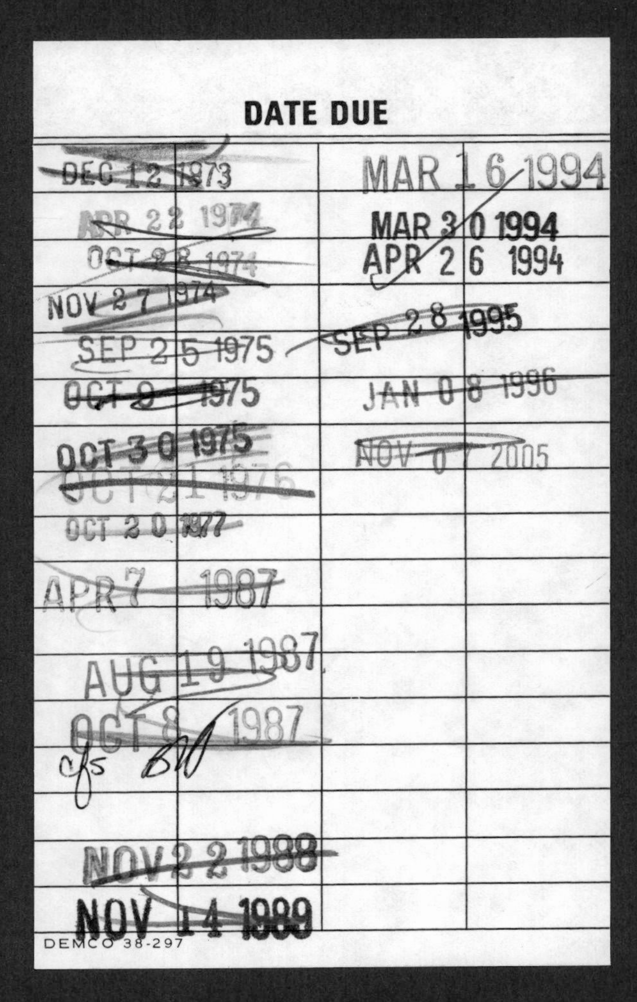